Housing Phenomena in Abuja, Nigeria

A CASE STUDY

DR. JOSEPH ALUYA

authorHOUSE®

AuthorHouse™
1663 Liberty Drive, Suite 200
Bloomington, IN 47403
www.authorhouse.com
Phone: 1-800-839-8640

First published by AuthorHouse 6/18/2008

ISBN: 978-1-4343-5599-7 (sc)
ISBN: 978-1-4343-6966-6 (hc)

Printed in the United States of America
Bloomington, Indiana

This book is printed on acid-free paper.

ABSTRACT

A qualitative, phenomenological study using a modified van Kaam method by Moustakas (1994) with audiotape and semi-structured transcribed interviews was conducted with a purposeful sampling of 30 individuals in Abuja, Nigeria. From the inductive experiences of the middle-income population, the study explored a lack of affordable housing as it affects the target population. To support and complement participant's responses from the qualitative interview questions, a five-point, Likert-type 25 quantitative survey questionnaires was administered to the participants. The research question was how does the lack of affordable housing impact the middle-income population? A lack of affordable housing was imperatively linked to double-digit interest rates attached to loans and the income range of the middle-income populations. Socioeconomic and stakeholders theories were used to conceptualize the concept of the lack of affordable housing. Research findings indicated that the economic infrastructure affects housing for the middle-income population. Because of the city's inadequate infrastructure development, a lack of affordable housing affects middle-income population (Bowditch & Buono, 2001; Newan, Ridenour, Newman, & DeMarco, 2003). The significance of study was to bring awareness to Nigerian leadership how the lack housing affects the middle income population. Recommendations for the stakeholders are to collaborate and seamlessly work to enhance technological information exchanges on housing. Externally, the International Monetary Fund, the World Bank Group, Habitat for Humanity, and the United Nations Educational, Scientific, and Cultural Organization to horizontally and vertically engage Nigerian banks to start granting low-interest loans for housing.

DEDICATION

I dedicate this study to Nigerians whom have followed same path and to my family (living and in heaven). To my mother- Iyawo Esther Ibhakhomu-Aluya in heaven, your grace, handwork, generosity, and kindness are all imbibed in me. Thank you mother, and your passing on to God's calling during my journal towards this terminal degree only strengthen me. Mother, your struggle in life to survive and to be a productive person in the society was also an inspiration for me. To my sister, Josephine Idedia, I dedicate present dissertation to you. Looking at our humble upbringing, the Almight God complemented us in a unique way. To my wife, Bibiana Aluya, I equally dedicate current study to you. Your contribution and support cannot be understated. Thanks for the three kids, which present study is dedicated. Justin, Brianna, and Chrystal, you are all wonderful kids and you were very supportive throughout this journey. Finally, I thank the almighty God for your guidance. In Isaiah 54:17. *No weapon formed against me shall prosper....* No one can take away your destiny. People might delay your destiny but our destiny is in our hands. Remember, you can always inspire to be the best you can possibly be. Even the rejected stone became the pillar of the house.

ACKNOWLEDGMENTS

First, let me acknowledge the Almighty God, the omnipotent and the omnipresent in our lives. Special thanks to my beautiful wife, Bibiana, your sacrifices, dedications, and devotions to the family cannot be overemphasized. You always insist that I finished whatever I started. Special thanks goes to my children, Justin, Brianna, and Chrystal, for the time which current project took from them.

Second, thanks to the Central Bank of Nigeria, especially the research department. The Central Banks employees' speed, efficiency, and effectiveness in which survey questions were answered and returned to me within a short period of time was unprecedented. I extend my appreciation to C. Omordi, C. M. Okafor, C. Anoya, and the entire Central Bank of Nigeria research department, Abuja. Thanks to Deputy Inspector General of Police (DIG) O. O. Onovo for providing an enabling environment to carry out this research. You are such a kind person and a transformational leader within the police force.

Third, thanks to A. Salihu of the Federal Capital Territory Administration (FCDA) and F. Bello for their help and directions in Abuja. Thanks to Alex Odiase for also helping in the collation of the research materials. Thanks to Alex and Bello for the research materials you collected from the participants. Finally, special thanks goes to those who have impacted indelible knowledge into me. How can you really thank people who impacted knowledge to others, but to say thanks? Thanks to Dr. T. Dasgupta., Dr. J. Bruns., and Dr. C. Barton. These intellectuals and academicians were the shinning light that guided my hands through a dark tunnel. I say thank you.

Contents

List of Tables

LIST OF FIGURES

CHAPTER 1:

INTRODUCTION

Affordable housing for middle-income populations represents an important part of the basic infrastructure necessary in the development of nations (Akinwale, 2004; Ibagere, 2002; World Bank Group, 2006). Ibagere noted that in the capital cities of developing nations, a "shortage of housing affects the middle-income population" (p. 3). One area known as the sub-Saharan African region had a population of over 600 million in 2004 and has continued to grow at a 10% annual rate (Taylor, 2000; White, 2005). The population was characterized by migrations from the interior regions towards cities because of socioeconomic pressures. As people migrated to the capital cities, housing prices increased, and the middle-income population could not afford housing (Al-Obaidan, 2002; Anugwom, 2001; Taylor, 2000).

In Abuja, the capital of Nigeria, only the rich can afford to purchase a home (Karley, 2003; Kenny, 2002; Le, 2002). Within the context of study, only the rich are referred to target population with an average yearly income of N185, 000, Naira, Nigerian currency ($1500 USD) (Akinwale, 2004; Ibagere, 2002; World Bank Group, 2006). Individuals with average monthly income of N12, 000 ($100 USD) or less are compelled to live in the city's suburban areas (Al-Obaidan, 2002). A phenomenological qualitative study on affordable housing was explored through the middle-income population "inductive experience" (Devers & Frankel, 2000, p. 2). From the middle-income people perspective, impact of the Nigerian culture, inadequacy in economic infrastructures on affordable housing are explored and explained (Moustakas, 1994, Strong, Ringer, & Taylor, 2001; Wren, 1994).

BACKGROUND OF THE PROBLEM

Nigerian people reside in a land equal to the size of California and Arizona in the United States combined (Country Reports, Nigeria, 2004). The centrally located city of Abuja was founded in 1976 and recognized as the official Federal Capital Territory Authority (FCDA) of Nigeria in 1991 (Ayemi, 2001; Ojide, 2003). Abuja was initially designed to cover an area of 250 square kilometers. In reality, Abuja is geographically located in an area of 8,000 square kilometers and has an estimated population of over seven million as compared to Nigeria's 140 million people (Country Reports, Nigeria, 2006; Ikejiofor, 1998). Nigeria is the largest country within the sub-African region with a combined population of over 600 million people in 2004 (Norris, 2001; Taylor, 2000). The World Bank Group (2003) has classified Nigeria as a poor nation. Regarding Abuja's affordable housing shortage, White (2005) suggested that it might be due to the lack of disposable income of middle-income populations rather than an actual shortage of homes.

Nigerian gross domestic per capita income was estimated to be $1,000 USD (World Bank Group, 2006). Under the study, the middle-income population consisted of employees whose monthly wages or salaries average an equivalent of $100 USD or less, which was equivalent to 12,000 Naira, the Nigerian currency. For the middle-income population, two thirds of the monthly income was typically allocated to purchasing food and renting a single-family house that averages $25 USD. Financial institutions, governmental agencies, and the private sector are all involved in the development of housing in Nigeria. In Abuja, Nigerian government allocated land for the construction of housing. Funds for housing are provided through financial institutions. The private sector builds homes. Functions of the financial institutions, governmental policies, and private are interchangeable within the context of understanding affordable housing. Financial institution, governmental agencies, and the private sector are described as the stakeholders (Cortright, 2001; Ekeogu, 2002; Mbeki, 1999).

A phenomenological qualitative research study explored a lack of affordable housing from the perspective of the middle-income population. An investigation into the lack of affordable housing in Abuja revealed that the supply of expensive houses exceeds the demand (Pindyck & Rubinfeld, 1989). Experts in strategic management indicated that leaders of financial institutions, governmental agencies, and the private sector strategies maintained high prices of homes in capital cities (Cascella, 2002; Gagnon & Michael, 2003; Mintzberg, Lampel, Quinn, & Quinn, 2003). Explored in the study are the middle-earners' point of view regarding the effects of stakeholders' (i.e., government, financial institutions, and the private sector) policies on affordable housing (DeSoto, 2000; Ibagere, 2002; Strong et al., 2001; Wren, 1994). Ibagere noted, "a lack of lower interest mortgage loans" (p. 3) explained how the supply of expensive houses exceeded the demand because many people could not afford housing.

Al-Obaidan (2002) studied 45 developing countries and posited that privatization of property reduced the inefficiencies inherent in public ownership. According to Al-Obaidan's findings, individual ownership of property stimulates a nation's economy. A deeper understanding of private property ownership as it affects the middle-income populations was necessary to explain the phenomenon of affordability of housing. DeSoto (2000) noted that allowing private ownership of real property might empower middle-income populations and improve economic conditions.

At the beginning of the 21st century, technology and its peripheral components have a role in the issue of affordable housing. Middle-income earners shared housing experiences regarding use of the internet while locating affordable housing. The internet usage and accessibility was not prevalent in the Nigerian housing market (Ahlawat & Ahlawat, 2006; Bayliss, 2002; Chowdhury, 2002). Information technology remained a vital component in the dissemination of housing profile materials to potential homeowners (Afuah & Tucci, 2003; Dai & Kauffman, 2002). One goal of the present research study was to explain the role of the internet in locating affordable housing.

A centralization of information into a single internet server in Abuja was an issue relevant to the present research study. According to the minister and mayor of Abuja, El Rufai (2004), stated that the purpose of having only one centralized server was to chronologically enter titles of landowners into a centralized database. Centralizing information into the Federal Capital Territory Administration (FCDA) server could help the Nigerian middle-income population in locating affordable housing (Bowditch & Buono, 2001; Davila, Gupta, & Palmer, 2003). In a city such as Abuja, it could be problematic to attempt incorporating the necessary technological components that lead to effective and efficient access to information about affordable housing (Ahlawat & Ahlawat, 2006; Chowdhury, 2002; Le, 2002).

STATEMENT OF THE PROBLEM

The middle-income population cannot afford housing in Abuja, Nigeria, and a lack of affordable housing contributed to a specific socioeconomic problem (Ayemi, 2001). Karley (2003) maintained that "higher interest rates attached to [the] loans" (p. 27) granted to middle-income earners through financial institutions have resulted in a housing shortage. Average income of Nigerians and the high interest rates applied to mortgages specifically relate to the problem of the shortage of affordable housing (Ayemi, 2001; Karley, 2003).

Shortage of housing for middle-income earners was an issue during Nigeria's authoritarian military leadership from 1970 to 1999 (Akinwale, 2004). In the first decade of the 21st century, the situation has not changed, and middle-income earners are still unable to locate affordable accommodations. Within the socioeconomic context, a lack of affordable housing is attributed to the macroeconomic approach in the management of the country (Akpan, 2003; Ayemi, 2001). Aderibigbe (2002) noted that Nigerian governmental policies from the 1970s to 2002 might have overlooked the core issue of affordable housing as it affected the middle-income population. Akinwale noted that the previous authoritarian governmental leaders overlooked the problems and the effects of affordable housing on the middle-income population in Abuja.

A qualitative design was appropriate for a phenomenological study. Explored in this study was the impact of affordable housing and housing shortage in Nigeria from the perspective of middle-income populations (Creswell, 2002). Ten middle-income earners from financial institutions, governmental agencies and the private sector were administered with semi-structured in-depth questions. There was face-to-face and paper generated interviews that followed the phenomenological approach to qualitative research. Questions were elicited from the participants' perceptions regarding individual experiences of the phenomenon of unaffordable housing.

A quantitative questionnaire that consisted of 25 questions constructed with a 5-point Likert-type scale (see Appendix A) supported the qualitative responses from the participants. Purpose of the questionnaire was to obtain (a) demographic information from the participants and (b) responses to questions about housing availability and affordability. Data from the survey questionnaire helped supported the qualitative interview data. Interviews and the survey were administered sequentially.

Moustakas (1994) explained that the experiences of the population under study might include subjective elements; internal validation became necessary through saturation of data. As part of the analytic process, the modified van Kaam methodology was used (Moustakas, 1994). A qualitative, phenomenological interview continued only as long as participants provided new and relevant information. Devers and Frankel (2000) noted that the qualitative research process is nonlinear and nonsequential. There were three core qualitative open-ended questions. A phenomenological study described and interpreted the experiences of middle-income earners regarding access to housing (Neumann, 2003; Simon, 2006).

Purpose of the Study

A lack of affordable housing was explored through the perceived experiences of the middle-income populations. A qualitative methodology and a quantitative survey questionnaire described and explained the lack of affordable housing as it affects middle-income earners. Qualitative research methodology was appropriate because of the nonlinear and nonsequential method of gathering data. Study was based on the perceptions of a phenomenon consciously experienced by middle-income populations. Data were collated from the financial institutions, governmental agencies, and the private employers. Stakeholders employ 90% of the middle-income earners in Abuja (Al-Obaidan, 2002). Samples were selected from the population of stakeholders for the interview. Survey questionnaires were administered to 30 individuals in Abuja (Creswell, 2002; Neumann, 2003; Simon, 2006).

Why the middle-income population is unable to afford housing in Abuja was explained in the study. Explored in the study was potential association between the lack of affordable housing for middle-income earners and the city's infrastructure development (Bowditch & Buono, 2001; Newan, Ridenour, Newman, & DeMarco, 2003). Specific group affected were the middle-income earners who live in Abuja and the suburban areas within the city (Akpan, 2003; Ayemi, 2001). The study was conducted in Abuja. Abuja has a population of over seven million and where 90% of the middle-income population is unable to afford housing (Ikejiofor, 1998). According to the Nigerian Minister of Housing, 16 million housing units are needed in Nigeria (Country Reports, Nigeria, 2004).

SIGNIFICANCE OF THE PROBLEM

Currently, significance of study was to discover a potential association between the lack of affordable housing and the policies that controlled the development of the nation's infrastructure. Ibagere (2002) noted that affordable housing represents a vital resource within a nation's economy, especially in a developing country such as Nigeria. A lack of affordable housing could significantly impact the socioeconomic status of the middle-income population in capital cities within the sub-Saharan African region (DeSoto, 2000; Wren, 1994). In the socioeconomic context, the study explained the consequences of stakeholders' policies regarding affordable housing (Boswell & Cannon, 2005). The study provided valuable information to the leaders of financial institutions and the private sector, and to the middle-income population in Nigeria.

Significantly, the study affected stakeholders' working synergies and the leadership styles. Leaders of the financial institutions, government agencies, and private sector might begin to work together to develop strategic to the housing shortage affecting middle-income populations. Stakeholders might come to view the lack of affordable housing through the prism, themes, patterns, revelations, and experiences of the middle-income population (Boswell & Cannon, 2005; Wolverton, 2003).

Finally, the study might provide valuable benefits in raising awareness regarding the use of technology to disseminate information about housing availability in Abuja (Bass, 1990; Bernstein, 1996; Wren, 1994). Dissemination of information on housing would benefit the middle-income population. With technology and the use of the internet, leaders in Nigeria would become better informed on affordable housing and the impact on the socioeconomic life of the country (Akpan, 2003; Huang, Chang, & Yu, 2006; Strong et al., 2001; Wolverton, 2003).

SIGNIFICANCE OF RESEARCH TO LEADERSHIP

Significance of the study was to inform Nigerian leadership of the phenomenon of a lack of affordable housing (Bass, 1990; Wren, 1994). First, the study explained the role of financial institutions regarding the lack of affordable housing for the middle-income population in Abuja. Explored in the study, were practices of banks creating a centralized server with the Central Bank of Nigeria (CBN) to verify credit, condition, capacity, collateral, and conditions for potential loan applicants. The CBN server could be linked to the existing Federal Capital Territory Authority (FCDA) server.

Second, a goal of the study was to demonstrate to the leadership of Nigeria the importance of governmental agencies working with the private sector on the issue of affordable housing. Last, the International Monetary Fund, the World Bank Group, Habitat for Humanity, and the United Nations Educational, Scientific, and Cultural Organization (UNESCO) could benefit from the study and help raise awareness of the socioeconomic problem of housing in developing nations. For example, the World Bank Group could assist leaders of developing nations in reducing housing shortages by channeling economic aid through housing programs. Similarly, Habitat for Humanity could provide low-interest construction loans and build affordable homes for middle-income earners in developing nations (Habitat for Humanity, 2005). The International Monetary Fund could financially assist stakeholders in Abuja, Nigeria.

NATURE OF THE STUDY

A phenomenological research design was applied in the study. Application of the research design allowed individuals to explain the effect of a lack of affordable housing in Abuja. A phenomenological qualitative research design was appropriate (Newan et al., 2003) to obtain first-hand accounts of the phenomenon of lack of affordable housing for middle-income earners. A quantitative survey questionnaire was appropriately used to complement the qualitative open-ended questions. Instrument used for the study was a modified van Kaam method by Moustakas (1994). A lack of affordable housing from the point of view of the middle-income population was explored in the study. Cooper and Schindler (2003) noted that a researcher begins with a description of the paradigm under study and follows with a secondary exploration through "gathering literature materials with data that are already available" (p. 152) in scholarly journals and peer-reviewed literature. Paradigm under study resulted in the documentation of data from the lack of affordable housing for middle-income populations. The data analyzed were based on the experiences of the respondents which indicated the main issue was middle income population's capacity to afford housing. The analyses revealed that it would be impossible for middle-income population to afford housing in the capital city without some form of housing subsidy.

Creswell (2002) recommended a triangulated design to analyze contrasting points and gain multiple perspectives that could be used to response or refute research questions. Data for analysis comes from (a) a survey of 25 questions on a 5-point Likert-type scale administered to a target segment population in Abuja, (b) semi-structured phenomenological interviews conducted with the same population, and (c) a review of relevant literature. Neumann (2003) noted that survey instruments administered to respondents could structurally lead to conceptualization, and the refined concept could then become a theoretical framework.

Middle-income employees from financial institutions, governmental agencies, and the private sector were the sample for the study. The middle-income population's place of employment and income as well as the ability of employers to provide housing subsidies was part of the criterion used in the sampling process. To understand the underlying mitigating factors that would decrease the housing shortage remained core to the study (Amit & Zott, 2001).

An overlapping similarity exists between quantitative and qualitative research methods (Creswell, 2002). A qualitative research method addresses the themes and the generalizations under study (Neumann, 2003). Themes in the current study were generated from interviews with three open-ended questions conducted with participants in Abuja (Creswell, 2002). Quantitative research methods condense data with precise measurements. In a questionnaire constructed with a 5-point

Likert-type scale, the respondents rated their degree of agreement with specific statements which reflected various themes relevant to housing shortages and housing affordability. Quantitative research methods are typically used to analyze relationships between dependent and independent variables (Simon, 2006). Data gathered for study were not quantified or validated through any causal relationship. For this study, data collated in the quantitative statistical analysis supported and complemented the participant's responses from the qualitative interview questions.

Primary data gathered in the proposed qualitative research explained the effects of a shortage of affordable housing on middle-income earners. In a phenomenological research, qualitative design was appropriate to discover the central themes, patterns, and constructs of the target phenomenon. A survey consisting of 25 questions on a 5-point Likert-type scale was used to obtain information on the central themes to complement the participant's responses from the qualitative questions. Nuances within the middle-income population' inductive experience affected the study findings, so there was careful interpretation of the data (Creswell, 2002; Neumann, 2003).

RESEARCH QUESTIONS

A phenomenological qualitative research study explored the lack of affordable housing from the experiences of the middle-income population. Research questions focus exclusively on the experience of participants or were developed through certain avenues that reconstructed a particular situation (Creswell, 2002). Exploring the common experiences of middle-income earners, shared culture, and how the shortage of housing impacts individual lives was primarily a qualitative design approach. Research questions focus on the housing shortage and the ability of the middle-income population to afford housing. Qualitative research questions are open-ended questions rather than specific or close-ended questions (Charmaz, 2006). The following research question guided the study: how does the lack of affordable housing affect the middle-income population in Abuja?

THEORETICAL FRAMEWORK

Theoretical framework of the proposed research study was based on stakeholder and socioeconomic theories. Friedman (as cited in Beauchamp & Bowie, 2004) noted, "the social responsibility of stakeholders is to increase profit" (p. 50). Stakeholders (i.e., government, financial institutions, and the private sector) objective centered on profit maximization. Profit maximization without understanding and addressing the societal problem of lack of affordable housing for the middle-income population would not lead to good social responsibility amongst stakeholders. Therefore, stakeholders' theories became crucial to the underlying conceptual framework of the study.

Fisher and Urich (1999) posited that all stakeholders must benefit from meaningful social programs. In the Philippines, for example, the government benefited through reduction of the overall costs of waterborne infections. The private sector reduced costs through eradication of water problems for the middle-income employees, (1) the financial institution benefited through government granted tax incentives and (2) capping the profit margin attached to loans granted to various villages for the supply of water (Fisher & Urich). Fisher and Urich's sociological philosophy on stakeholder theories guided study. The government, financial institutions, the private sector, and subsequently, the middle-income population would benefit potentially from successful social programs in Abuja.

Pertinent to the current study was Maslow's (1943) theory of the hierarchy of needs. According to Sumerlin (1997), Maslow constructed the theory of self-actualization in 1954. Maslow further expanded on the robustness of his theory in 1968, 1970 and 1971, and later included the five steps to self-actualization. Included in the steps were series of achievements before reaching the stage of self-actualization: the physiological, safety, love, and esteem need's comes before the optimal need of self-actualization (Sumerlin).

Maslow's theory consists of satisfying the physiological, safety, love, and esteem needs before self-actualization can occur. Definition of self-actualization is the instinctual need for people to make the best of self-abilities and strives to be the best (Sumerlin, 1997). Maslow's theory consists of satisfying the physiological, safety, love, and esteem needs before self-actualization can occur. Middle-income populations in Abuja would not strive to be the best without resolving the issues of housing. Paramount to the study, housing for the middle-income population leads to self-actualization. Without housing for the middle-income population, the physiological, safety, love, and esteem needs might not be met (Sumerlin).

Within the private sector, the lack of affordable housing for the middle-income population was the phenomenon under study. Herzberg's (1964) motivation-hygiene concept will be used as a theoretical backdrop to describe the lack of affordable housing for private sector employees. Based on Herzberg's hygiene theory, middle-income employees perform at an optimum capacity, and a lack of affordable housing was inextricably intertwined with daily functions (Chowdhury, 2002). Paradoxically, Nigeria is classified as a poor nation, yet rich in oil and natural resources (World Bank Group, 2006). From the perspective of the middle-income population, housing subsidies or lower interest rates might be the means to affordable housing.

As a result of the study, the expectation was for the Nigerian government leadership to adopt new housing policies. In the expectancy theory, Mangelsdorff (2001) noted a particular governmental effort might lead to a particular first-level outcome such as explaining the issues of housing shortage. Turner (2002) maintained that the punctuated equilibrium model (i.e., a theory of evolutionary biology applied to social and political contexts to explain sudden changes in policy after long periods of inaction) could be applicable to bureaucratic governmental policies that might result in a short-term radical change in the housing industry.

Assumptions

Study explored the lack of affordable housing through the perceptions of the middle-income population. Employees in governmental agencies, financial institutions, and the private sector participated in the research. An assumption for the study was respondents would provide honest and credible information during the process of administering the qualitative interview questions.

LIMITATIONS

Participation in the study was limited to individuals who agreed to participate voluntarily. The study was limited to the number of subjects interviewed and the amount of time available to conduct the research. Generalizability of the study was limited to middle-income families in Abuja, Nigeria. Finally, the study was limited by the validity and reliability of the instruments used.

DELIMITATIONS

Explicitly, focus of the study was limited to the middle-income population's capacity to afford reasonable housing in Abuja. Other cities in Nigeria are excluded from study. The scope included affordable housing for the population under study and the housing industry in Abuja. Participants were governmental employees, staff at financial institutions, and employees within private organizations (Jones, 2003; Kacena, 2002).

SUMMARY

A lack of affordable housing through the middle-income population perception was explored in this study. A phenomenological qualitative study explored how the lack of affordable housing affects middle-income earners. Chapter 1 began with an introduction to the study, followed by discussions of the background, problem statement, purpose, significance, nature of study, and research question. Research question that guided the study was: how does the lack of affordable housing affect the middle-income population in Abuja? A modified van Kaam method by Moustakas (1994) was used to analyze and synthesize responses from the qualitative questions posed to participants.

A section of the chapter included an overview of theoretical frameworks. Paradigm under study was the middle-income population capacity to afford housing near places of employment. A lack of affordable housing by middle-income population was interlinked to the nation's infrastructure and the policies that dictated its development. The governmental agencies, financial institutions, and the private sector are stakeholders within the phenomenon of shortage of affordable housing. Houses are available and might remain vacant because only the rich can afford housing in Abuja. Chapter 2 will provide a review of the literature on the socioeconomic and stakeholder issues involved in the topic of interest.

CHAPTER 2:

REVIEW OF THE LITERATURE

A lack of affordable housing from middle-income population's perspective was explored in this study. Purpose of the phenomenological qualitative study explained how a lack of affordable housing affects the middle-income population in Abuja. Chapter 2 starts with an overview of germinal theories about stakeholders. Literature for the study was presented with the following subdivisions: (a) documentation of searches, (b) overview of theoretical frameworks, (c) literature on affordable housing for the middle-income population, (d) governmental policies, (e) stakeholder theories, (f) private sector, (g) electronic marketplaces, (h) communication, (i) literature on culture, (j) summary and conclusion.

DOCUMENTATION

Materials for the study are documented and would be saved in a bank volt for three years. After three years, the materials will be destroyed. Materials used in the study were from scholarly journals, texts, and scholarly manuscripts. Literature materials on stakeholder theories were downloaded from the electronic libraries. EBSCOhost research database provided 9,000 articles, of which 7,000 were peer-reviewed articles, and 53 of the peer-reviewed articles were used in the study.

Research material on stakeholder theories regarding housing development and financial institutions in Nigeria were difficult to find. The internet provided information regarding housing availability and affordability in Abuja. In Nigeria, housing development information was used to corroborate information gleaned from financial institutions.

Nigeria's national web site provided information on stakeholder theories, leadership issues, and leadership styles.

Another area of macroeconomic literature materials that proved difficult to locate electronically was literature on the terminology *middle-income population,* nebulously defined, and what it means to different segments of the population. One developing nation interprets the phrase middle-income population differently from another developing nation. Literature materials regarding middle-income earners were difficult to research due to the disparity in economics and the standard of living used as a benchmark in defining the middle-income population in Abuja. Macroeconomic indicators suggested different formulas of classifying and defining the middle-income population (World Bank Group, 2003).

THEORETICAL FRAMEWORK

Germinal socioeconomic theories of Maslow (1943) and Smith (1776/1976b) guided the analysis. Housing shortages or a lack of affordable housing for middle-income earners in Abuja was the social economic phenomenon explored in the study. Maslow's theory was important to the proposed study. Maslow constructed the theory of self-actualization in 1943 (Sumerlin, 1997). In the theory, physiological, safety, love, and esteem needs come before the optimal need of self-actualization. Central in the review of the literature for the study was the first level of Maslow's theory, which related to 90% of physiological needs of the middle-income population. Physiological needs are related to the 90% of the population in Abuja that are unable to meet the basic necessity of the housing (Country Reports, Nigeria, 2006; Ikejiofor, 1998).

Focus of the investigation was affordable housing that was the physiological needs for units of study. Matteson and Ivanevich (1999) noted that Maslow's physiological needs included affordable housing for employees' comfort. Housing was a basic necessity for all populations. In Abuja, the middle-income earners are particularly affected by the lack of affordable housing near places of employment. If the middle-income earners' needs are not met, the next level of Maslow's pyramidal hierarchy of needs was difficult to reach. Low-interest construction and mortgage loans to middle-income earners through financial institutions were means to offer middle-income earners a level of safety.

Trigg (2004) claimed that Maslow's pyramidal hierarchy of needs is not a scientific, clinically researched, and empirical study. Trigg contended that human needs are insatiable, and Maslow's pyramidal hierarchy of needs does not reflect the reality of human needs nor, according to Hanley and Abell (2002), do human needs occur in the order of Maslow's pyramidal sequences. Some individuals give priority to better pay, transportation, and healthcare benefits instead of affordable housing.

Herzberg's (1964) motivation-hygienic theory consisted of the "motivators and the factors that lead to dissatisfaction at work also known as the hygienic factors" (Wren, 1994, p. 333). Two aspects of the theory deals with motivation, such as better work environment, better vacation rather than increased employee's salary, and the hygienic aspect of the theory that deals with internal motivation. Employees with reasonable accommodations may produce better in a place of work (Wren). In the theory, incentives such as housing, vacation, a better work environment, better healthcare to employees could lead to higher productivity rather than increased salary. Motivators in the theory relates to the possibility of employers conjecturally providing housing for employees. Employers who inculcates housing scheme for employees increased productivity (Wren).

A review of Herzberg's (1964) hygienic factors pointed to the motivational aspect of employers in providing housing to middle-income employees. Housing incentives as a motivator for employees lead to an increased in productivity and employee retention. In the context of Herzberg's theory, housing incentives for middle-income earners have more importance than other hygienic factors such as achievement and recognition. Furthermore, DeSoto (2000) posited that the policies for mortgages and construction loans are crucial factors in explaining the lack of affordable housing in Nigeria.

DeSoto (2000) explained "the mystery of capital [and noted the reason] why capitalism triumphs in the West and fails everywhere else" (p. 1) is that mortgage rates and construction loans have been granted to middle-income earners in developed nations over many generations, and the funds continued to circulate through the system.

Conversely, in developing countries, the lack of borrowing power for the middle-income population has led to a lack of housing infrastructure and socioeconomic hardship. As noted in Matteson and Ivanevich (1999), Maslow's theory of self-actualization supports DeSoto's theory that explains the importance of mortgage and construction loans for the middle-income earners (as cited by Wolverton, 2003). Wolverton contended that without construction or mortgage loans, developing nations remain poor due to an inadequate infrastructure. Wolverton noted that the middle-income population and small businesses sustain the capitalistic economy in developed nations. Another reason housing shortages might persist in developing nations was that financial institutions grant *defunct* loans (i.e., loans that a bank cannot afford to make and that lead to the bank's closure).

Wolverton (2003), in reference to DeSoto (2000), explained that capitalism fails in developing nations because of inefficiency and overly inflated prices attached to housing. Wolverton further noted that capitalism fails in developing nations due to financial institutions overpricing and overfunding. Wolverton noted that loans and mortgages attached to residential properties do not reflect accurate appraisals of the properties. Consequently, defunct loans have resulted in the liquidation of some financial institutions in Nigeria.

Liquidation of financial institutions resulted in a complex chain of events that placed enormous pressures on the economy and the market forces in Abuja. Numerous events that led to the breakdown of the Nigerian economy occurred in other developing nations (Osili, 2004). According to Osili, the strain on Nigeria's economy because of bank failures resulted in financial distress to the financial market despite Nigeria's substantial oil and natural resources.

HOUSING FOR THE MIDDLE-INCOME POPULATION

Ibagere (2002) noted that the Nigerian governmental bureaucracy was responsible for the lack of affordable housing for the middle-income population in Abuja. According to Ibagere,

> [housing represents] an important sector of the economy and an index of its economic advancement, prosperity, and investment in real estate development. Housing remains a major contributor to the physical assets of

a nation. Mass housing represents shelter provided for the masses—the greater part of the people in a nation. (p. 1)

Ibagere (2002) maintained that Nigerian governmental bureaucracies stifle the housing market for the middle-income population. Bureaucracy prevented middle-income earners from owning homes. Ibagere contented that bureaucracy explained how various decrees on housing policies did not ease housing shortages or improve affordable housing in Abuja.

Ibagere (2002) contended that past military governments promulgated housing decrees that were policies burdened by bureaucracy failed to improve the housing situation. Present Nigerian leadership might be open to addressing the concerns of a lack of affordable housing (El Rufai, 2004). Presently, for example, a centralized server partially maintains data regarding housing owned by individuals in Abuja (El Rufai, 2004). In Nigeria, government allocates land and financial institutions funds the private sectors in building housing for the middle-income earners, and these programs are still at the infancy stage (El Rufai, 2004).

Weber's bureaucratic theory explains how "differences in authority were based on differences in the beliefs by which legitimacy is attributed to an authority relation" (As cited by Scott, 2003, p.44). In developing nations, bureaucracy create situations were the majority of the population tends to gravitate towards the leader in authority (Ferraro, 2002). In developing nations, the leaders' shortcomings are conjecturally legitimatized. In Nigerian, for example, people sought special favors from leaders in order to by pass the bureaucracy association with land allocations. The Nigerian leaders in return, would only allocate land for building houses to people of interest (Brown, 2004).

According to Brown (2004), bureaucracy in Nigeria has led to the problem of *godfatherism*. Land allocations in Abuja are assigned to people due to influence and connection to authority. Brown claimed that part of the Nigerian bureaucracy system could explain why housing shortage exists. Scott (2003) asserted that Weber's bureaucratic theory, in which economic and sociological concerns are juxtaposed, could possibly be intertwined to the problems of housing shortage.

In Nigeria, financial institutions' expediting applicant's home loan package explained how individuals navigate through the bureaucracy by appeasing the authority (Brown 2004). In the private enterprise, employers' encountered how bureaucracy inhibits capacity to build homes. Matteson and Ivanevich (1999) noted that Weber's typology advocated that "control is an efficient element in the efficient functioning enterprise" (p. 131). Weber's agenda for bureaucracy is also sociological. The Nigerian leaders legitimized authority to control how land allocation is distributed to the middle-income population. Explanation of housing shortages in Abuja relates to the sociological aspect of understanding how people in authority allocate land to the middle-income populations.

Matteson and Ivanevich (1999) noted that Weber's typology advocated that "control is an efficient element in the efficient functioning enterprise" (p. 131). Weber's agenda for bureaucracy is also sociological. Explanation of housing shortages in Abuja relates to the sociological aspect of understanding how people in authority allocate land to the middle-income populations.

Matteson and Ivanevich (1999) explained that Weber's theory is based on an analysis of bureaucracy in the developmental sense. Weber's bureaucracy is characterized by the existence of charismatic, traditional, and rational–legal types of authority. Alternatively, if the leaders in Nigerian adopt the leadership traits advocated by current study, perhaps the middle-income population could own homes.

Weber's particularistic authority diffuses linear structures embedded in the system and consequently tends to impede change in organizations. Contextually, Weber's particular bureaucratic structure might compound the shortage of affordable housing for the middle-income population. A lack of affordable housing for middle-income earners in Abuja might be tied to a particular bureaucratic system that does not provide the means to reduce housing shortages in Nigeria.

Akinwale (2004) offered insight regarding issues of housing shortages and affordability that result from failed governmental decrees. The past Nigerian military government enacted but did not enact decrees to ease housing problems. Akinwale noted,

> the housing shortage for the masses resulted in the creation of the National Housing Fund (NHF) under the policy of decree number 53 of 1989, decree number three of 1992, and federal mortgage bank degree number

82 of 1993; these decrees were to help facilitate the loans
for the low-income people. (p. 5)

Nigerian military governmental decrees failed to address the effects
of a lack of affordable housing for the middle-income population because
the decrees were not implemented (Akinwale). Akinwale maintained
that the actions of the military leaders through the formulation of
decrees did not enhance and encourage collaboration and formation of
partnerships among stakeholders in the housing industry.

GOVERNMENTAL POLICIES

Governmental policies reflected on the Nigerian leadership styles
and ingrained culture that explained reasons for the lack of affordable
housing (Bowditch & Buono, 2001; Schein, 2004). For instance, the
Nigerian Minister of Housing and Urban Development indicated that
16 million housing units are needed in Nigeria (Country Reports,
Nigeria, 2004). The Nigerian government leadership was assumed
to have put in place initiatives that could help mitigate the lack of
affordable homes for the middle-income population. Leadership
styles that inhibit affordable housing remain either authoritarian or
transactional (Akinwale, 2004).

Bass (1990) noted, "Authoritarian leaders depend on power and
ability to coerce and persuade" (p. 419) people to carry out goals. Past
authoritarian leadership styles of the Nigerian government and the lack
of enactment of housing decrees negatively affected the middle-income
population (Akinwale, 2004). Bass posited that the transactional
leadership style lies between the transformational and the authoritarian
approaches. Currently, leadership style practiced by the government
in Nigeria in the early 21st century can be described as transactional
(Bass, 1990). With an effective leadership style, leaders in Nigeria
could persuade and inspire stakeholders to collaborate in addressing
housing issues affecting the middle-income populations. Conjecturally,
transactional leadership style has not produced such collaboration.

Stakeholders' collaborative efforts were inhibited by the Nigerian
housing policies of 1994 (Ibagere, 2002). The National Housing
Policies organization was to produce over 121,000 new housing units
for Nigerians. Private financial institutions, individuals, states, and
governmental agencies, namely the Ministry of Works and Housing

and the Federal Housing Authority (FHA), were expected to develop partnerships. Past military leaders' policies could not encourage affordable housing for the middle-income population because of the authoritarian leadership and practices in Nigeria (World Bank Group, 2000). Although the government was expected to subsidize housing, stimulate infrastructure development and provide inexpensive land, none of the goals were achieved. Partnerships between the private sector, government agencies, and financial institutions failed. For instance, government employees were able to resell to private parties at highly marked-up prices the inexpensive pieces of land received (Ibagere, 2002).

According to the World Bank Group (2000), home ownership ratios have been between 20% and 40% of the total population of over 135 million people in Nigeria. Financial institutions' inability to grant low-interest loans to middle-income earners possibly results in the lack of affordable housing in Abuja. Middle-income population's inability to access low-interest loans through banks explained the lack of affordable housing that severely affects the population. Economic infrastructures needed to provide loans to the middle-income population are not in place (Ayemi, 2001). Strong infrastructures create an environment conducive to Nigeria's overall development.

Democratic leadership of Nigeria was established in 1999. Recapitalization of a minimum deposit of 25 billion naira ($185.2 million USD) required by the CBN in December 2005 could have led to the formation of stakeholders' partnerships and produced affordable housing in Abuja (Nigeria Central Bank, 2005). According to the FHA's housing policy (Country Reports, Nigeria, 2004), financial institutions required the middle-income population to deposit 50% of the total purchase price for a house and pay the balance in a 5-year amortization period. Interest rate on the mortgage balance ranges from 11% to 13% amortized over 5 years.

Bukley (as cited in Bass, 1990) posited that a successful democratic leader is "a person who crystallizes on what the people of his or her country need or desire and illuminates the rightness of desires by effectively coordinating and achieving the stated objectives" (p. 23). Democratic leaders in Nigeria are not willing to formulate housing policies that meet the needs of the middle-income population. If the leaders are not properly educated about the importance of affordable housing in relation to the nation's economy, Nigerian leaders would continue to prevent the creation of effective policies.

Ibagere (2002) claimed the lack of improvement in the affordability of middle-income housing is due to governmental bureaucratic policies. Scott (2003) maintained that when Weber's bureaucratic system is used, it leads to the creation of a particular type of structure that could impede housing affordability. According to Ibagere, decrees promulgated by the Nigerian leadership and governmental policies to ease the housing shortage failed due to the structure of the Nigerian system. Brown (2004) noted that policies in Nigeria are continuously undermined due to the practice of favoritism, nepotism, and tribalism. Housing shortages were to be abated by the Nigerian government. Reasonably, abatement of housing shortages was not within the scope of the present research. Reasonable efforts from the Nigerian government leaders should expectably lead to a reasonable positive outcome, and the efforts may be embedded in the expectancy theory (Mangelsdorff, 2001).

According to expectancy theory, a probability exists that a particular governmental effort will lead to a particular first-level outcome (Mangelsdorff, 2001). Nigerian leadership was expected to promulgate housing decrees and make conscientious efforts in implementing the decrees. Past Nigerian governmental efforts could continue to affect the actions of stakeholders. For example, the past Nigerian government efforts to implement housing policies through housing decrees were not effective (Ibagere, 2002). The Nigerian housing decrees are still embedded in the process of individuals acquiring land in Abuja despite technological innovative methods currently being adopted (El Rufia, 2004). Actions through governmental efforts illustrated that subsidization of housing and granting low-interest loans to the middle-income population failed. Government agents or employees might still be undermining conscientious efforts advanced by the Nigerian leadership. To ease the housing shortage, the new democratic government should formulate realistic and practical plans. Such plans could eliminate bureaucratic measures that prevent financial institutions from granting low-interest loans payable over a reasonable number of years (Ibagere, 2002).

The invisible hand theory (Smith, 1776a, 1776b) explained how governmental actions and policies might indirectly be affecting the economy of a nation. The government of a nation may for instance enact housing policies to enhance housing policies for the middle-income earners. By contrast, the actions of the government were contrary to the policies. Nigerian leadership's actions conjecturally hindered implementing the housing policies from proposal to fruition. In Nigeria, the actions and policies of the government in relationship to housing affected housing. If change does not occur within the Nigerian government, the economy of Nigeria will continue to be negatively affected. Government employees' actions can be said to illustrate the invisible hand theory of Adam Smith (1776/1976b).

Edna (1997) analyzed the historical foundation of the invisible hand theory credited to Smith (1776/1976b). According to Edna, David Hume and Adam Ferguson (as cited by Edna, 1997) should be credited with the philosophical foundation of the invisible hand theory, along with Smith. Edna posited the invisible hand theory was a result of Hume and Ferguson "stumbling upon establishments, which are indeed the result of human actions, but not the execution of any human design" (p. 187). Smith was credited with elaborating the theory and coining the phrase *invisible hand* (Edna, 1997, p. 1). Smith's invisible hand theory might be used to explain the Nigerian government's actions with respect to housing for the middle-income population. By omission or by design, housing shortages or a lack of affordable housing exist in Abuja.

Smith (1776/1976b) posited, "The rent which goes to support the vanity of the slothful landlord, is all earned by the industry of the peasant" (as cited by Edna, 1997, p. 35). Elliot (2000) maintained that Smith's (1776/1976b) interpretation of rent collection by landlords is inextricably linked to poverty associated with the middle-income population. Subsequently, the doctrine of rent collection from the middle-income population in Abuja, when extrapolated from Smith's theoretical construct, explained how a lack of affordable housing exists for the population under study. Suggestively, if the middle-income population cannot afford to rent, substitution for mortgage payments would be impossible.

Samuelson's (1961) theory of nonsubstitution of price is also applicable to the current study (as cited in Garegnani, 1983). Substitution theory stated that a middle-income population sees no rationality in substituting rent payments with mortgage payments for home ownership without an increase in income if renting was still possible. In the private sector, one can surmised that when wages increased, middle-income earners would prefer owning homes rather than renting, within the context of the current theoretical framework. Middle-income population would prefer to use the opportunities coming from an income increase to obtain healthcare benefits instead of affordable homes. Alternatively, the middle-income population considered a marginal income increase an incentive to provide more food for the family rather than to own a home.

Ricardo (1961) offered that a determinant of housing demand and supply is the sustainable equilibrium price over a period. Ricardo described effective demand theory as people's ability to pay for particular goods and services at a point in time. Middle-income population's ability to pay for housing, irrespective of the availabilities and vacancies was explained within the stakeholders' working synergies. Smith (1776/1976b) stated that the ability to pay is determined by the price. Ability to pay is also determined through the *invisible hand* of the Nigerian government. According to Klein (2003), Smith's (1776/1976a) revealed the invisible hand of the government might lead to both negative and positive economies of scale. The invisible hand of the Nigerian government in formulating housing policies led to a rise or fall in the standard of living for middle-income earners in Abuja.

Wren (1994) posited that a nation's standard of living depends on the policies of the government regarding the nation's infrastructure. Social programs formulated through the Nigerian government's policies are crucial in explaining the economic emancipation of the middle-income population. Implementation of social programs was ineffective and inefficient due to bureaucracy. Klein (2003) noted, "Weber's typology on bureaucracy in conjunction with favoritism, nepotism, and tribalism" (as cited in Brown, 2004, p. 14) may lead to ineffectiveness and redundancy in governmental policies.

The Country Reports (2004) reported corruption, nepotism, and favoritism prevented the Nigerian system from building an adequate number of affordable housing units. The minister and mayor of Abuja, El Rufai, revoked and reissued certificates of occupancy to land owners in Abuja. According to El Rufai (2004), certificates of occupancy were revoked due to previous Nigerian authoritarian leadership styles and governmental policies that failed to address the housing shortage and the lack of affordable housing. Understandably, the minister was entering housing data and information from particular areas into an FCDA centralized server (Nigeria Central Bank, 2005). Nigerian leadership and governmental housing policies are factors that prohibit stakeholders' working synergies.

STAKEHOLDERS

Stakeholder theories emerged and became prominent in the 1970s (Andriof, Waddock, Husted, & Wells, 2002). Post et al. (2002) noted that stakeholder theories date back to the 1920s during the rejuvenation of General Electric in the United States. Stakeholder theories focus on employees, managers, shareholders, customers, and the public. Focus of the theories was satisfying stakeholders' needs and wants, which was pivotal to sustainability and longevity of any business, any organization, or any governmental social programs (Bowditch & Buono, 2001; Charreaux & Desbrieres, 2001; Newstrom & Davis, 2002; Schermerhorn, Hunt, & Osbuorn, 2003).

Jonker and Foster (2002) defined stakeholder as "any group who can affect or is affected by the achievement of the firm's objectives" (p. 188). In Nigeria, stakeholders might oppose the integration of real estate information into an FCDA centralized server. Nutt (2004) posited that stakeholders' opposition could be antagonistic and even problematic for any meaningful integration of changes. Change agents, referred to in the agency theories as the principals, and the reluctance to change are at the core of the housing market problems (Nutt, 2004). Affected stakeholders might determine that technology does not meet or exceed individual needs. Understandably, stakeholders are profiting and benefiting from the lack of affordable housing affecting the middle-income population. Figure 1 describes the interrelationships of the stakeholders.

AVAILABILITY OR LACK OF AFFORDABILITY

Fisher and Urich (1999) noted that when stakeholders established partnerships, social programs were more likely to be implemented, resulting in economic benefits. Fisher and Urich offered that the implementation of social programs (e.g., as a water project in the Philippines) in developing nations could not be realized without funds granted through stakeholders in the private sector.

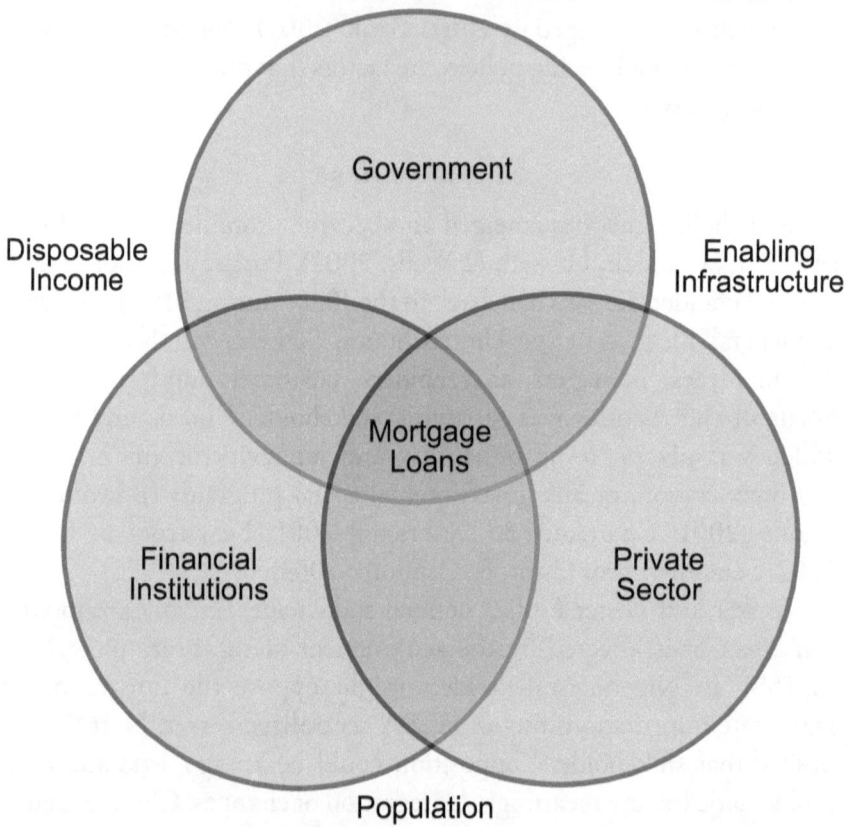

Figure 1. Collaboration of stakeholders

In Abuja, *horizontal and vertical* collaboration of stakeholders would lead to a successful housing program that in turn, result to affordable housing. Horizontally, financial institutions could collaborate with other similar institution locally. Local or national financial institutions collaboration would be based on similar interest. Similar interest could be in formed of lowering mortgage interest rates attached to loans granted to the middle-income population. Vertically, international financial institutions could be integrated with local and national institutions with an objective of lowering interest rates on loan granted. Profit would be inculcated as an addition incentive within the vertical and horizontal collaborations of the stakeholders.

Attaching profits to social programs such as housing motivates stakeholders to understand the need to collaborate in the housing schemes. Although, Friedman (as cited in Beauchamp & Bowie, 2004) asserted that the "social responsibility of the stakeholders is to increase profits for its [*sic*] shareholders" (p. 50). Financial institutions, the private sector, and the Nigerian government would still benefit from social programs such as housing. Stakeholders would work synergistically to maximize profits, while all sundries in housing schemes would benefits from a social responsibility of granting lower interest loans to middle-income population.

Poverty in Nigeria explained how a lack of affordable housing affects the middle-income population in Abuja (Aderibigbe, 2002; Obadan, 2002). In the past, stakeholders made no concrete effort to collaborate in order to understand the existence of housing shortages (Obadan, 2002). Poverty amongst the middle-income population explained why the lack of affordable housing in Abuja exists. An increase in income of the middle-income population might alleviate the economic hardships and lead to affordable housing.

Private Sector

Literature review on the private sector included economies of scale and employees' retention or the employment of the middle-income population within private enterprise. To increase economies of scale and employees' retention in the private sector becomes imperative to describe affordable housing as an incentive to the middle-income population. Tortola (2001) related retention of employees to (a) an emotional security, (b) the need to be appreciated, (c) the need to be included, (d) the need to be celebrated, (e) economic security, (f) good wages, (g) job security, and (h) the need to be understood. Tortola further delineated affordable housing and reasonable wages for the middle-income population. Reasonable wages for the middle-income population are equitable to the standard and cost of living in Abuja. With reasonable wages, the middle-income population acquires the options of renting, leasing, or owning a home. In addition, the use of electronic marketplaces, effective communications, and technological infrastructures would alleviate the hardship of searching for available housing.

Within the Nigerian financial institutions, banks are stakeholders. Actions of the banks could prohibit the collaborative efforts of other stakeholders within the housing industry if not properly aligned internally. Moldoveanu and Martin (2001) maintained that banks often could not match titles to properties. Moldoveanu and Martin determined that in developing cities, banks might be incapable to mine data ownership of land or houses from a centralized location. Nigerian banks such as the United Bank for Africa and the First Bank Place in Nigeria have a connectivity rate of 98% between various branches; the banks have no connections to the housing industry (Al-Obaidan, 2002). Banks, as stakeholders in Nigeria's financial market, lacked the capacity to grant low-interest construction or mortgage loans to the middle-income population (DeSoto, 2000; Gee & Burke, 2001; Kenny, 2002).

Literature review on financial institutions indicated that the banking industry have no access to housing information in the open or private network. For instance, the CBN's or FCDA has no centralized server for housing that could make housing transactions efficient. Decree Number 53 of 1989, which empowered licensing private mortgage insurances (PMIs) to finance houses, was not enacted. According to CBN (Country Reports, Nigeria, 2004), 195 PMIs were licensed, 74 PMIs sent returns to CBN, and 124 PMIs remained dormant or ineffective. In 2005, CBN consolidated banks with a capitalization of 25 billion naira. Banks capitalization created a solid financial market in the private housing sector (Country Reports, Nigeria, 2004).

Karley (2003) posited that basic criteria for granting loans to potential borrowers, namely, "credit, capacity, capital, collateral, and conditions" (p. 30), could become a general assessment test. Figure 2 depicts the general assessment test that could be used by financial institutions. Financial institutions could apply Karley's general assessment test locally, nationally, and globally.

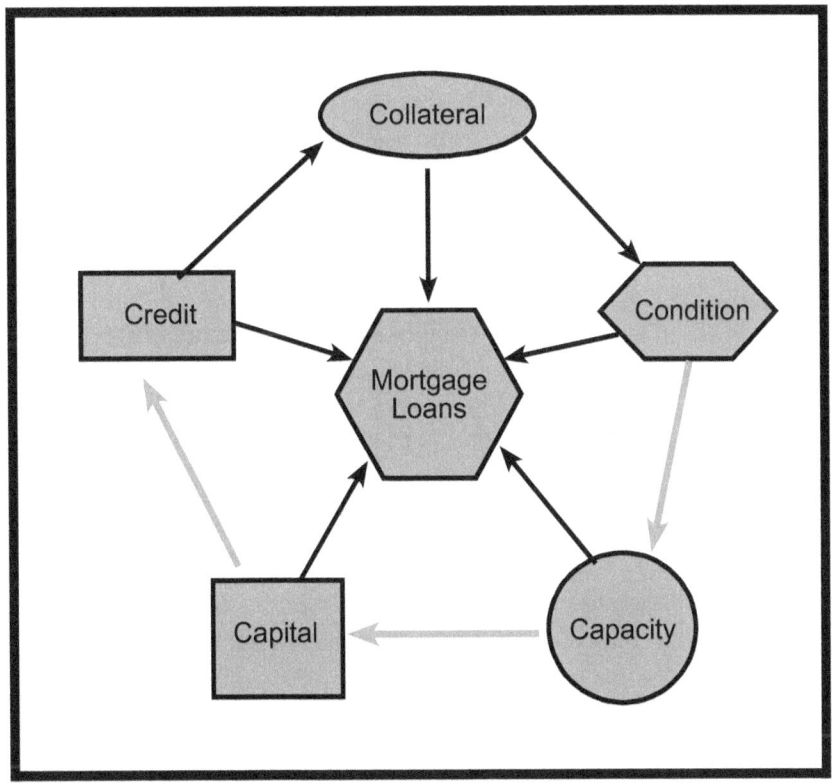

Figure 2. General assessment test

In Nigeria, financial institutions might be incapable in meeting the practical criteria required to grant low-interest loans based on the general assessment test in Figure 2 (Chowdhury, 2002). The onus should be on the stakeholders (i.e., the Nigerian government, the private sector, and financial institutions) to formulate a model that explores how low-interest construction and mortgage loans would directly affect the middle-income populations. Forming strategic alignment between stakeholders would create affordable housing (Becker, 2002).

ELECTRONIC MARKETPLACE

Revealed in the literature review, electronic marketplaces and the supply of electricity needed for housing transactions are sporadic (Adenikinju, 2003). Adenikinju reported that 20% to 30% of initial investments in the private sector were for procurement of materials to augment the supply of electricity. Adenikinju noted that without a supply of electricity and the proper infrastructure (i.e., the internet connectivity) to support the electronic marketplace, finding available houses on the internet would be impossible. Analysts in information technology suggested that from the platform of the electronic marketplace, efficiency, complementarities, lock-in, and novelty will expedite finding availability of affordable homes (Akpan, 2003; Amit & Zott, 2001; Ekeogu, 2002; Moore, 2002, Peter & Donnelly, 2003). Electronic marketplace allows real estate brokers to facilitate renting, buying, and selling homes through the electronic medium. Rappa (2004) referred to present medium of transactions transmitted on the electronic marketplace as the brokerage model.

The brokerage model explained stakeholders' working synergies that facilitate the search for properties available to rent, sell, or buy for the middle-income population (Afuah & Tucci, 2003; Gottschalk & Abrahamsen, 2002; Rappa, 2004). Afuah and Tucci and Rappa believed the brokerage model would increase the economies of scale in a developing nation's economy. In the brokerage model, brokers charge fees to help facilitate housing transactions. Brokers' roles are incorporated in business-to-business (B2B), business-to-consumer (B2C), or consumer-to-consumer (C2C) markets (Broadbent & Kitzis, 2004; Duru, 1997).

Trickle-down effects of the brokerage model create economies of scale in developing nations and help the middle-income population conduct a search for a home. Medium of communication from one computer server to another was an important aspect of the issue of affordable housing for the middle-income populations. Communication of information via horizontal and vertical integration with brokerage models in congruence with factors that could enhance stakeholders' working synergies could alleviate housing problems in Abuja (Ariba, 2000).

Amit and Zott (2001) offered that four advantages derived from e-businesses are (a) efficiency, (b) complementarities, (c) lock-in, and (d) novelty. Efficient e-commerce in real estate includes instant access to information and the delivery of information to middle-income earners looking to buy homes in Abuja. A trickle-down economic effect increased the economic power of Nigerian middle-income earners.

Buyers and sellers have a wide range of options in selecting houses for lease or purchase from e-businesses.

Suggestively, transactions cost in the housing industry remained high due to the dissemination of asymmetrical information on housing to customers. In macroeconomics, the customer was assumed to benefit when complementary goods are available due to symmetrical information on availability (Amit & Zott, 2001). Lock-in and novelty result in relationship marketing based on the satisfaction and patronization of the middle-income population within the new paradigm in housing transactions (Akpan, 2003). Conjecturally, with centralization of information and housing information dissemination, the middle-income population benefits from the different properties that are available and affordable. In relationship marketing, for instance, customers who are satisfied with a particular type of housing transactions may tend to want to use the same type of method in future transactions (Amit & Zott, 2001).

COMMUNICATION

With the global proliferation of technology, effective communication and feedback loops are pivotal to any nation's economic survival. Communication enables stakeholders' working synergies. Communication can affect how information on availability and affordability of housing for the middle-income population is disseminated. Ehikhamenor (2003) described the historical evolution of the computer and its functionality within Nigerian financial institutions.

Ehikhamenor analyzed the genesis of computers as a model of communication starting in the 1960s and developing into network servers in the 21st century. Ehikhamenor's statistical analysis suggested that 40% of banks had connectivity capacity. Connectivity rate for banks increased from 40% to 90% because of the capitalization of 25 billion Naira (Nigerian Currency) the CBN required from financial institutions (Nigeria Central Bank, 2005). Despite the capitalization, information on the availability and affordability of housing are not readily accessible on the internet.

The internet was created in the United States in the 1960s for defense projects. In 1979, three students in North Carolina opened the internet to the public (Dearnley & Feather, 2001). Eventually, Paul Baran, an American engineer, was credited for the invention (Dearnley & Feather). In Abuja, electronic marketplaces are not used to locate ready-to-occupy apartments and available or affordable houses (Akpan, 2003; Groves, 2004; Kubasek, Brennan, & Browne, 2003).

Real estate brokers in Abuja might not be electronically connected to available real estate properties. Afuah and Tucci (2003) claimed that the electronic marketplace increased the effectiveness and efficiency of searching for affordable properties. Establishing electronic marketplaces, according to Clinton (2000), would provide digital opportunities for employment, trigger the economic emancipation of the poor, and might help mitigate finding available housing.

Abuja's citizens are unable to locate the availability of potential properties on the internet for either buying or leasing. Harvey (1989) called the internet *a distance of spatio-temporal compression* (as cited by Akpan, 2003). Gottschalk and Abrahamsen (2002) referred to the internet as the globalization of the marketplace. Establishment of electronic marketplaces, virtual kiosks, and malls in Abuja would ease the housing shortage by providing information about houses that are affordable or available at any point in time. Interlinking and integrating the internet with real estate properties would reduce search time for middle-incomers buyers. Analysts in information technology suggested that developing nations could imitate and adopt the strategies of internet communications that exist in the United States in cities such as Abuja (Gadde & Hakansson, 2001; Khalil & Hazem, 2005; Strange, 2005; Truong, 2004).

According to Guillen and Suarez (2005), the digital dilemma is related to developing countries' social and political contexts and policies that lead to inadequate access to technology in searching for properties on line. Guillen and Suarez proposed that developing countries with limited or no internet accessibility for the middle-income population make it impossible to locate available homes on the internet. Guillen and Suarez emphasized the contrast between developed nations' capacity to connect to high-speed internet as well as extranet and intranet networks and developing nations that have virtually no access to the superhighways. Guillen and Suarez noted that problems in the digital world resulted in an increased search time for housing in countries where connectivity to the superhighways is limited and unstable. The fundamental new tenet in communication is that the internet has replaced traditional methods of gathering information, locating the availability of housing, marketing, and exchanging information on properties (Akpan, 2003; Mbeki, 1999; Norris, 2001; Phillips, 2002; Truong, 2004).

Another factor that hindered stakeholders' ability to work synergistically was the market aggregate economy of developing nations. Effective electronic communication lead to market aggregation that can eventually overcome market fragmentation and that increased buyers' ability to have more choices (Block & Catfolis, 2001; Le, 2002; Truong, 2004). Le and Truong stated that supply chain efficiencies, transparency, and collaboration between firms resulted from market aggregation. Middle-income population ability to make choices regarding the type of accommodation provision needed was important. According to Porter (1990), technological tools have given an effective and efficient competitive edge to end-users. Centralization of property within the FCDA could facilitate finding available and affordable housing in Abuja.

In Abuja, the centralization of housing information in a server within the FCDA would ease the search for housing for the middle-income population. Scott (2003) explained that efficient and effective methods of arriving at solutions occur when "information becomes centralized rather than decentralized" (p. 50). Pioneers in technological innovative methods of information centralization concurred that property information would be easily available through a centralized server (Guetszkow & Simon, 1955; Leavitt, 1951; as cited by Wren, 1994). Franz (2003) referred to the concept of information technology as the artificial intelligence described by Simon (1955) as the framework for explaining human intuition. Centralization of information in a server or system cannot be de-emphasized (Wren, 1994). Vroom noted, "centralized structures more rapidly organize to solve problems. Participants in peripheral positions send information to the center of the networks, where a decision is made and sent out to the peripheral" (as cited in Scott, 2003, p. 162).

Despite the advantages of information centralization as an economic characteristic applicable to finding affordable housing, disadvantages do exist. According to Truong (2004), electronic marketplaces emerged as avenues of exchange for goods and services. Electronic marketplaces also contributed to the foreclosures of emerging electronic businesses. Perils are associated with electronic marketplaces. Rapid rise and fall of electronic marketplaces explained why firms are reluctant to use electronic marketplaces method for transaction (Truong, 2004).

Other economic characteristics emerge with the centralization of information. Information on potential middle-income earners could be stored in a customer relationship management database (CRM). Customer relationship management systems (CMS) could open avenues for middle-income earner credit profiles and other pertinent information to be used for potential home-buying processes. According to Payne, Christopher, Clark, and Peck (2000), CRMs and CMSs have been used for relationship-marketing strategies with respect to housing. Banks and other financial institutions in Abuja could use data mining for economies of scale, and middle-income earners could start using the CMS to facilitate housing search in Abuja.

Lafferty, Goldsmith, and Newell (2002) maintained that the dual credibility model was derived from a centralized system with CRMs and CMSs in a server. With the centralization of information in the FCDA server, consumer attitudes might not be influenced in real estate transactions because the system would be efficient. Efficiency system does not lead to change in the Nigerian culture that prohibits individuals from obtaining loans.

Nevertheless, government leaders in Abuja would endorse the use of a centralized information system of properties in an FCDA server. In a centralized real estate system, information on housing and affordability data are stored in a centralized location. Financially, the storage of information in a centralized CBN server gives credibility to potential homebuyers. By logging into the centralized server, potential real estate buyers could start locating properties.

Technology use was an important element within the stakeholders' working synergies. Turban, Lee, King, and Chung (2000) explained, "Disintermediation is the process of eliminating intermediaries in real estate transactions" (p. 63). The internet components such as intranet and extranet have become sociological tools to eliminate intermediaries from real estate transactions. Turban et al. noted re-intermediation would start occurring when buyers in the city of Abuja are able to navigate through electronic malls and start locating properties online. Middle-income earners in Abuja will use the online medium to locate and make offers on homes. Symmetrical information and communication using technology would expedite an efficient home search.

Drucker and Peters (2002) suggested that without technological information, no business or government agencies could survive the 21st century. As contemporary writers in management and information systems, Drucker and Peters asserted that the world was a global village connected electronically through technology. In the 21st century economy, global electronic village are linked futuristically with the internet, extranet, and intranet. Abuja city could belong to the global electronic village (Malone, Yates, & Benjamin, 1989).

Becoming linked with the global village would require the establishment of an electronic marketplace in the city, and the environment in Abuja could be transformed to accommodate an electronic marketplace (Baron, 2003). Electronic global village would serve as a means of understanding and mitigating the problem of lack of affordable housing and how it affects the middle-income earners (Annan, 2001; Clinton, 2000). The internal and external cultural mechanisms that created a housing shortage marginalized middle-income populations by denying them access to the advantages of the electronic medium. In the literature reviewed, analysts agreed that stakeholders in Abuja are not disseminating technological information on housing availability or affordability to middle-income earners (Afuah & Tucci, 2003; Drucker, 1998; Khalil & Hazem, 2005).

In addition to the internet, the working synergies of the private sector and governmental agencies could increase competition through the dissemination of information to the middle-income population. Imperfect competition in the Abuja housing industry impedes an optimum potential profit in the private sector. Most information on the housing shortage and affordability was not disseminated through technological information systems. Analysts in information technology concur that for a housing industry to become profitable and effective from the standpoint of access, information dissemination on available and affordable homes should be made accessible to the affected constituents (Cortright, 2001; Ekeogu, 2002; Mbeki, 1999).

Technology enhanced the working relationships between the stakeholders towards creating affordable housing. Technology could increase the income per capita of Nigerians living in Abuja if the stakeholders integrate technological information into the housing system (Afuah & Tucci, 2003). Consequently, economic characteristics such as an increase in employment and an increase in wages would affect income. A competitive advantage emanated from technology usage in the real estate industry. Such a competitive advantage would increase per-capita income of the middle-income population. When the per-capita income of the middle-income population increased, homes would be affordable. Scholars have suggested that the internet and its technological components would provide the middle-income population with useful information on housing availability and affordability (Lipis, Villars, Byron, & Turner, 2000; Truong, 2004).

CULTURE

Culture is defined as a set of assumptions, values, norms, and tangible signs or artifacts as well as the facilitation of people's intrinsic and extrinsic social behaviors, ethnicity, language, and subliminal coded messages within enterprises (Appelbaum, Shapiro, & Elbaz, 1998; Kanungo, 2001; Luthans, 2005; McNamara, 2001; Schein, 2004). A lack of affordable housing can be explained through the cultural motifs embedded in the culture within which the stakeholders operate. Nigerians could be uncomfortable accepting loans from financial institutions to construct single-family residences because of culturally ingrained beliefs. Within the Nigerian culture, a myth existed that people who used low-interest loans to build homes might be financially insolvent.

According to Appelbaum et al. (1998), the internal and external factors in the diverse culture of Nigeria could be related to the lack of affordability of housing. For instance, Nigeria has over 350 languages and 250 ethnicities (Country Reports, Nigeria, 2004). Appelbaum et al. defined culture as four-dimensional parts: (a) high power distance and low power distance, (b) high uncertainty avoidance and low uncertainty avoidance, (c) individuality and collectivity, and (d) masculinity and femininity. In Abuja, the patrilineal culture minimizes the power of the female population and of the middle-income earners from owning homes. Understanding the patrilineal culture in Nigeria might help understand how a lack of affordable housing affects the population under study.

Ferraro (2002) noted that stakeholders could cultivate a particular type of cultural mindset that would alleviate the problem of affordable housing. The government's position and policies formulated as a mechanism to create affordable housing in Abuja have been unsuccessful (Ibagere, 2002). According to Ferraro, culture alone cannot explain a phenomenon. Nigerian leaders as stakeholders would need to incorporate a substantive actionable vision and a global mindset to explain a lack of affordable housing. Paradigm shift in a global mindset would culturally be realigned with a strategic global vision.

Brown (2004) maintained that governmental policies of favoritism, nepotism, and tribalism are part of the Nigerian culture and maintain the lack of affordable housing for middle-income earners. Brown noted the failure of Nigerian governmental policies could be due to *godfatherism*, which occurs when lower staff members are given favors in lieu of senior staff to the disadvantage of the majority. Under godfatherism, lower staff members can bypass official policies. Policies can also be intentionally misinterpreted and misrepresented to the lower staff employees' benefit. Consequently, the misinterpreted unwritten policies might explain the lack of affordable housing and how it affects the population. Nigeria could inferably be a collectivistic culture where group behaviors usurp individual behaviors (Hollenbeck, 2000; Kagitcibasi, 2001).

Barrera (2001) described collective bargaining theory. Collective bargaining power of the middle-income earners in Abuja, if effectively used, would alleviate the lack of affordable housing. Team members could pull resources together to establish policies that would help creating access to affordable housing for the middle-income population. Barrera noted that collective bargaining affects the demand and supply of products. In Abuja, teams and the collective efforts of middle-income earners could lead to affordable housing.

Summary

This study explored the lack of affordable housing through the experiences of the middle-income population. In the literature reviewed, culture and values within the Nigerian society were described as elements that affect how the stakeholders act towards the housing problem. The established leadership culture and values explained the lack of affordable housing and how it affects the middle-income population. Experts on the phenomenon of culture as it affect leaderships indicated that the established leadership culture dominant in Nigeria existed in other developing nations (Eccles & Wigfield, 2002; Kacena, 2002; Schein, 2004). Research study used various theoretical frameworks within the housing market that suggested why there was a lack of affordable housing and how it affected the middle-income population in Abuja, Nigeria.

Fisher and Urich's (1999) stakeholder theory explained the need for the Nigerian government, financial institutions, and private organizations to profit in any social program from proposal to implementation. The literature review included Smith's (1776/1976b) invisible hand theory, Maslow's (1943) self-actualization theory, and Herzberg's (1964) two-factor theory. Within Nigerian governmental policies, Ibagere (2002) offered insight into how formal governmental housing decrees to establish affordable housing failed.

In the review of the literature on the private sector, economic characteristics were communication, the electronic marketplace, and the invisible hand of the Nigerian government. Literature review indicated that the Nigerian government's culture, when placed in proper perspective, conjecturally explained why home ownership was not accessible for middle-income earners. Adenikinju (2003) noted that affordable housing was a core infrastructure for the development of a nation, and affordable housing for middle-income population was conspicuously missing in Abuja. The literature review revealed that the current governmental administration was gradually establishing a housing program in Abuja (Adenikinju, 2003).

CONCLUSION

This study explored the lack of affordable housing through the experiences of the middle-income populations. For any meaningful development to occur in developing nations, the issue of affordable housing should be addressed (Ibagere, 2002). Housing programs remained the core competency and domain of a nation when it comes to infrastructure development. Developing nation capacity to provide affordable housing for its masses was the focus of the present study. Affordability of housing for the middle-income population contributes to the economic development of Nigeria. The literature review revealed that in the new city of Abuja, housing development would represent prosperity, the economic emancipation of middle-income earners, and infrastructure development. Chapter 3 describes the research design chosen to facilitate data collection and analysis for the study.

CHAPTER 3:

METHOD

This study explored the lack of affordable housing in Abuja, Nigeria, through the perceptions of the middle-income population. A qualitative phenomenological research study was to purposefully understand how a lack of affordable housing affects middle-income population. Sample size included 30 individuals who work in governmental agencies, financial institutions, and the private sector. Semi-structured interview questions, and a survey questionnaire were administered to the participants. A modified van Kaam method by Moustakas (1994) was used to analyze and synthesize data collected from the research questions. Responses from the survey questionnaires supported the analysis from the qualitative research questions posed to participants.

In Chapter 1, the research question asked: how does the lack of affordable housing affect the middle-income population? Chapter 2 reported and discussed the literature relevant to the phenomenon (i.e., lack of affordable housing for the middle-income population). Newan et al. (2003) explained that the overall purpose of a study dictates the type of design and methodology. Chapter 3 describes the qualitative research design and the appropriateness of the selected design. Topics included in the chapter are the selected population and sample frame. Confidentiality, geographical location of study, instrumentation, data collection, data analysis, validity and reliability are topics discussed, captioned by the summary of the chapter.

RESEARCH DESIGN

A qualitative research design is the process of collecting, analyzing, triangulating, synthesizing, interpreting, and reporting data (Creswell,

2002). In the current qualitative research study, three open-ended questions were administered to participants. A modified van Kaam method by Moustakas (1994) was used for this study. To support the qualitative questionnaire, a 5-point Likert-type scale was administered to 30 participants who are employees of governmental agencies, financial institution, and the private sector in Abuja. Experts in real estate management, financial and strategic planners helped support, refute or complement responses from the participants. A qualitative phenomenological research design was chosen because the people who experienced unaffordability and unavailability of housing could best described the impact (Moustakas, 1994; Salkind, 2003). Another source of data were survey questionnaires used for ranking and in obtaining demographic information. Participants' ranking of 25 statements that related to the variables uncovered in the literature review explained the lack of affordable housing. Participants ranking of the 25 statements were primarily used to support the qualitative interview questions.

Appropriateness of Design

A qualitative phenomenological design was appropriate for the study because it allowed the participants to describe a phenomenon experienced (Creswell, 2002). A phenomenon was the impact of a lack of affordable housing on the middle-income population. Qualitative designs are suited to the exploration of social, economic, and psychological phenomena from the perspectives of those who experienced or have experienced the phenomenon. Moustakas (1994) described the phenomenological design methodology as the gathering of primary data that provided insight on the "lives involved, or who were involved, with an issue" (p. 7). Under current study was the lack of affordable housing in Abuja, Nigeria, and how it affected the middle-income population. Middle-income populations provided and described the phenomenon based on personal experience, culture, income, and socioeconomic status (McNamara, 2001; Schein, 2004; Strange, 2005).

Qualitative research method included three open-ended questions that generated the themes and generalizations (Creswell, 2002; Neumann, 2003). No intention to determine causal or correlational relationships, or used précised measurements and statistical analysis in order to define relationships between dependent and independent variables (Simon,

2006). Data in quantitative research are used to quantify and validate causal relationships between the variables. Because quantitative survey questionnaires were administered to the participants to support the qualitative responses does not suggest a mix method design.

A qualitative phenomenological research method is nonlinear and nonsequential (Devers & Frankel, 2000; Page, 2004). Devers and Frankel noted that a qualitative study is appropriate to access the inductive experience of the participants. A 5-point Likert-type with 25 questions was used to complement and support responses from qualitative questionnaires. Introduction and the use of quantitative statistical analysis conjecturally do not lead to a mix methodology in the study. Quantitative analysis supported, expanded, explained, and complemented responses from the qualitative interview questions. Samples included individuals who belong to the population of middle-income employees. Within the categories under study, people described the lack of affordable housing as part of a nation's infrastructure development. Participants were employees purposefully selected from governmental agencies, financial institutions, and the private sector. Individuals shared different perceptions of the phenomenon as understood. A qualitative research design was appropriate for the study (Simon, 2006).

RESEARCH QUESTIONS

A phenomenological qualitative research study explored the lack of affordable housing from the experiences of the middle-income population. Moustakas (1994) noted that capturing the perceptions of a population and the participants' inductive answers to the research questions helps explained the phenomenon under study. Focus for study was how affordable housing remained vital to a nation's infrastructure development. For the study, the research question was: how does the lack of affordable housing affect the middle-income population? Qualitative research questions are open-ended questions rather than specific or close-ended questions (Charmaz, 2006).

POPULATION

Population sampled resides in the city of Abuja. Participants included 30 middle-income earners whose places of employments are located in central Abuja. Pertinent to the study was the middle-income earners' ability to rent homes in proximity to place of employment. Sample population provided rich information on housing affordability and availability to middle-income earners. In a qualitative phenomenological research study, the expectation was to interview no more than 30 participants in the city of Abuja. Cooper and Schindler (2003) noted that qualitative research requires a small sample size that ranges from 10 to 30 participants.

Participants were selected based within salary range (\$100 to \$700 per month), five years length of stay in Abuja, and two years individuals experience in finding housing accommodations. Another criterion for the selection process was whether or not participants' employers subsidized housing or provided housing for employees. The sample included ten participants from financial institutions, ten participants from governmental agencies, and ten participants from private organizations in Abuja. Employees in governmental agencies, the private sector, and financial institutions provided pertinent information regarding housing affordability. Participants are expected to describe aspects of housing availability and individual ability based on experience in obtaining construction and mortgage loans.

Informed Consent

Specific middle-income population employers received letter of introduction describing the study and requesting permission to conduct interviews and administer a short questionnaire to employees (see Appendices A & B). Based on Neuman's (2003) recommendations, the letter provided a succinct and clear description of the study and an explanation of the rationale for conducting the research. Prospective participants were fully informed of the purpose and procedures used to complete the study. Individuals were made to understand the benefits of contributing to the research study as well as complete freedom to participate voluntarily and without any coercion. Participants were made to be aware of no risk associated with participations.

Sampling Frame

Sample population was drawn from the middle-income earners in Abuja's government agencies, financial institutions, and the private sector (Cooper & Schindler, 2003). Specific criterion for the sample frame selection was salary range. Excluded from the sample frame were employees whose rents are subsidized or provided with housing accommodations from the selection process. Individual experiences in finding available and affordable housing accommodation were critical to the selection process. A few executive staff within the target population was included in the sample frame. Units of analysis for the study were governmental agencies, financial institutions, and private sector organizations.

CONFIDENTIALITY

Information gathered during research study were filed and stored in a banking volt. The data will be stored for three years. After three years, the data will be destroyed. Information regarding the participants will be kept in confidence. Before the participants participate in the interviews, individuals were assured that privacy and confidentiality would be strictly maintained. Since the data was based on the personal experiences of the participants, it was of the utmost importance to uphold all ethical principles, including confidentiality.

GEOGRAPHIC LOCATION

The study took place in Abuja, the capital city of Nigeria. Information was gathered from governmental agencies, financial institutions, and private organizations located in Abuja. Financial institutions such as the Central Bank of Nigeria, First Bank Place of Nigeria, and other banks within five-square-miles of the Central Bank of Nigeria and First Bank Place of Nigeria were solicited for participation. The Ministry of Housing and Works employees, Federal Development Investment Capital employees, and FHA employees received materials pertaining to the study. Employees from other private organizations and governmental agencies participated.

INSTRUMENTATION

Instrumentation for the qualitative phenomenological research study used was a modified van Kaam Method by Moustakas (1994) with tape-recorded and transcribed semi-structured interviews with selected participants. The research instrument was used to address the core research question of how does the lack of affordable housing affect middle-income population in Abuja, Nigeria. Seven steps that guided the process of analyzing narrative data as advocated by Moustakas (1994) are:

1. Listing and preliminary groupings

2. Reduction and elimination of invariant constituents and repetitive responses

3. Clustering and categorizing core themes

4. Checking the invariant constituents and their related themes against the participants' information

5. Conducting an individual textural description of the experience

6. Constructing an individual structural description of the experience

7. For each participant of the study, construct a textural-structural description of the meanings and essences of the experience (Moustakas,

   1994).

As part of the analytic process, the modified van Kaam methodology was used (Moustakas, 1994). Coding of data occurred when categories, themes, and patterns were discovered. In addition, the coding process helped determined information through review of the literature for similarities in other studies that supported the emerging themes. Current qualitative phenomenological research design used the experiences and perceptions of the middle-income population to describe the phenomenon. Data collection was semi-structured interviews with open-ended questions (Moustakas, 1994). Three open-ended questions prompted participants to share experiences with access to affordable housing near place of employment. Other interview questions that are within the delimiters were administered to participants. Questions that were used in the phenomenological interviews are:

1. Based on your experiences, how does the lack of affordable housing affect the middle-income population in Abuja?

2. Based on your experiences, how does the Nigerian culture impact the price on housing in Abuja?

3. Based on your experiences, how does technological information exchange within the stakeholders in Abuja result in availability of housing for the middle-income population?

Quantitative questionnaires were administered to participants to support the qualitative responses. Step one was administering the interviews to the participants using the seven steps as advocated by Moustakas (1994). Step two was gathering the demographic questionnaires. The second process consisted of administering survey questionnaires to participants. The survey questionnaires consisted of 25 statements on a 5-point Likert-type scale with anchors from *strongly agree* to *strongly disagree* (see Appendix A). Explored in the study was a lack of affordable housing and how it affected the middle-income population in Abuja, Nigeria. Invariably, statements on the survey questionnaire were formulated using information from the literature review. Statements included the most pertinent variables in the topic of lack of affordable housing in Abuja as described in Chapter 2.

Data collection instruments provided cognitive, experiential, and behavioral data regarding the middle-income earners' capacity to reside in Abuja (Creswell, 2002; Hair & Bush, 2003). Respondents' knowledge regarding the housing industry in Abuja was vital. Respondents' experience about housing affordability in Abuja was to the understanding of the phenomenon of interest. For this study, the behavioral type data was whether or not respondents intend to rent or buy a home in the city.

DATA COLLECTION

Data was collected from employees of government agencies, financial institutions, and private organizations located in Abuja. First, permission to conduct the research was requested and given by the stakeholders. Second, the meetings were set-up at the employees' official premises. Third, the meetings took place during working hours. Fourth, participants introduced themselves. After the introduction, the purpose of the research was explained to the participants.

During the explanations, those who are eligible were selected. Purpose of the research study was described; the voluntary nature of the study and participant confidentiality was explained. Participants were free to choose whether or not to participate. Data was gathered in a central location in Abuja. A qualitative interview provided rich data (see Appendix B), and a questionnaire will provide demographic information and rankings of statements on the housing affordability. For a qualitative study, an assumption into phenomenological study was that the research questions become the primary instrument for data gathering (Creswell, 2002).

DATA ANALYSIS

Qualitative analysis software aligns disciplines for a structured, repeatable and validated approach to analyze data. QSR Nvivo7® is highly recognized computer based qualitative research analytical tool. In interpreting qualitative data, the computer based analytical tool was designed to handle data gleaned from the study. Data was analyzed by coding themes into the qualitative software, QSR Nvivo7® in this study. The software helped the research process to discover and describe the text-based structural patterns. Contextual elements that contributed to a deeper explanation and understanding of the various themes became explicit. Moustakas (1994) outlined the following three steps for systematically analyzing qualitative data gathered in the phenomenological study:

1. *Horizontal Analysis - Listing and preliminarily grouping,* which is referred to as horizontalization. Horizonalization refers to the giving of equal value to every statement directly relating to the question asked.

2. *Structural Analysis - Reduction and elimination.* The various blocks or nodes of information defined from the horizontalization step are organized into logical grouping and subgroups. Within this context, the research process determines the invariant themes through testing each expression for two requirements: a) if it contained the essence of the experience, and b) if it could be labeled. Overlapping expressions that are irrelevant are deleted. Items

that remained will be identified as the invariant themes of the experience.

3. *Contextual Analysis.* Textural or conceptual implications and conclusions can be analyzed after data arrangement. Explored are themes, threads of information, and concepts that involve deeper analysis than the simplified presentation in a matrix or tree structure.

Data analyses are ongoing processes that start when data are collected (Creswell, 2002). During data analyses, information from the interviews was examined and the content analysis performed by experts in estate management in order to discover common themes. Taken into consideration were the variables of income, length of stay, and intention to stay in Abuja. Research materials were documented and coded. Percentages were calculated based on the raw data from the questionnaire. Informatively for the study, the portion of the survey questionnaire based on the 5-point Likert-type scale provided a means to support participant's qualitative responses.

VALIDITY AND RELIABILITY

Validity refers to how a researcher tests the intended variables being measured, and reliability refers to accuracy, precision, and dependability of the measurement (Cooper & Schindler, 2003). In a qualitative phenomenological research study, the instruments of data collection directly targeted the variables that described the phenomenon of lack of affordable housing for the middle-income population of Abuja, Nigeria. One expert in the field of real estate management and strategic policy planning was consulted to verify the internal validity and reliability of the information gathered from the respondents. Expert was chosen based on (a) level of education (Master's degree or level 19, level 19 is ranked executively as a permanent secretary of a governmental agency), (b) having at least ten years in their profession as consultants, and (c) having been residents in Abuja for at least 15 years. Three experts for this study agreed, disagreed, or remained neutral to the opinions of the participants. One expert in real estate management responded to the same qualitative interview questions and quantitative survey questionnaire as other participants. Results from the experts supported, refuted, or remained neutral to the opinions and responses to questionnaires posed to the middle-income population.

External validity refers to the generalizability of findings to other populations. There was no expectation that the results of the study applied to populations outside Abuja. Some degree of generalizability exists for populations with similar characteristics in other developing nations. Expectation in the study was that participants would provide credible accounts of experiences. Validity and reliability of the findings depended on whether or not the respondents understand the importance of providing truthful accounts of experiences and perceptions of the phenomenon of interest.

To further validate participant's responses, research questions that did not directly relate to the lack of affordable housing were not included in the textual descriptions as guided by step four of the Moustakas (1994) modified van Kaam method of analysis. Step four specifics that invariant constituencies "not relevant to the co-researcher's experience be deleted" (p. 121). Data presented in the textural description was relevant to the experience as tested and validated through the research methodology. Creswell (2002) explicitly identified threats to validity and reliability and potential weaknesses in the research design. Using the QSR Nvivo7® software and the three step process to analyze and synthesize data, thus offered constructive discipline to support data validation and reliability.

SUMMARY

Chapter 3 described the phenomenological methodology for the proposed study. A qualitative phenomenological research design fulfills the goals of the research. A lack of affordable housing and how it affects the middle-income populations of Abuja, Nigeria, was the phenomenon under study. Using the modified van Kaam method of analysis by Moustakas (1994), data presented in the textural description was relevant to the experience as tested and validated through the research methodology.

Due to nature of the problem that dictates methodology used, study design was appropriate (Creswell, 2002). Three open-ended qualitative questions provided information that explained the phenomenon. Other similar questions within delimiters were used to further explain the phenomenon (see Appendix B). In addition, the questionnaire provided demographic information and ranked opinions regarding the relevant variables in the topic of lack of affordable housing. In participant's responses, research questions that did not directly relate to the lack of affordable housing were not included in the textual descriptions as guided by step four of the Moustakas (1994) modified van Kaam method of analysis. Data presented in the textural description was relevant to the experience as tested and validated by the research methodology. A Likert-type scale was used to analyze and rank the levels of how a lack of affordable housing affects the middle-income population. Quantitative survey questionnaires serve to complement and support participant's responses from qualitative interview questions. Sample size consisted of 30 participants in Abuja, Nigeria. Chapter 4 reports the details of the research findings.

PRESENTATION AND ANALYSIS OF DATA

This study explored the lack of affordable housing for the middle-income population in Abuja. Organization of Chapter 4 centered on the thematic research question identified in Chapter 1. Explicated in Chapter 2 was the literature review for current study. Chapter 3 detailed the method of the qualitative phenomenological study and research design and why it was appropriate. Population selection strategy, data gathering process, method of data validation and reliability were described in Chapter 3.

Chapter 4 presents findings from the study. Quantitative survey questionnaire was administered to participants to primarily support and complement responses to the qualitative questions. Chapter 4 starts with the selection of the sampling procedure, methodology and data analysis. Within the findings sub-captioned are the general overview of study, clustering and thematizing, and qualitative and quantitative data analysis. Saturation of the phenomenological study, research questions, themes, summary and conclusion are congruently discussed.

Sampling Procedure

A letter of introduction was sent to prospective employers stating the intent of study. A letter of introduction also created an avenue to present the consent forms/letters to employees with the employers' permission. Throughout the survey process, participants gathered in an official conference room at the work site or at a cafeteria convenient to the participants' place of work.

METHODOLOGY

Cooper and Schindler (2003) noted that qualitative research requires a small sample size that ranges from ten to 30 participants. There were face-to-face interviews that were conducted with 30 participants, who were active employees of financial institutions, governmental agencies, and the private sector. The discussions with the interviewees were tape-recorded. Participants were recruited from three groups: the Central Bank of Nigeria Abuja (CBN), the Federal Capital Development Authority (FCDA), and the private sector. The CBN staff was surveyed first at a conference room in the Central Bank building. Private sector employees met at a local restaurant convenient to all participants. FCDA participants met at the FCDA conference room. Similar procedures were conducted with all groups. A pre-interview session was conducted to develop a sense of rapport with all participants.

On arrival at Abuja, the researcher contacted the executive manager regarding the pre-arranged meeting at the Central Bank of Nigeria (CBN) headquarters. After a brief discussion, the objective of the meeting was explained. In the Research and Statistics Department of CBN Abuja, the head of the department invited the participants into a conference room during working hours. In the conference room, 13 participants were gathered. Purpose of the research study was described; the voluntary nature of the study and participant confidentiality was explained. Three employees were dismissed for not meeting the study criteria. Four criteria were used to select participants: (a) participants earned a salary between $100 and $700 USDA, (b) participants have lived at least five years in Abuja, (c) participants have attempted to find housing accommodations at least twice, and (d) employers did not subsidize or provide housing for employees. In the study, ten CBN employees agreed to participate.

Similar protocol was observed with the Federal Capital Development Authority (FCDA) employees. Sixteen FCDA staff gathered in the official conference room. After some discussion regarding the nature of survey questions, six of the participants were dismissed for not meeting the set criteria. Within the FCDA, ten participants completed survey questionnaire.

In the private sector, employees from different businesses located in the same vicinity were invited to a local cafeteria. Through individual managers within the private sector, 18 participants were informed of the pre-arranged interview. After explaining the purpose of the study, the voluntary nature of the study, and participant confidentiality, eight private sector employees were dismissed for not meeting the study criteria. Those employees whose houses were subsidized were not eligible to participate. Private sector participants were ten who completed the survey questionnaires.

Three experts participated. Experts were chosen based on (a) level of education (Master's degree), (b) having at least ten years in their profession as consultants, and (c) having been residents in Abuja for at least 15 years. A real estate management expert was met during working hours. Discussions centered on real estate trends, including affordability of housing for the middle-income population. Similar protocol was observed with the financial consultant and the strategic planner. Discussion with the financial consultant anchored on the rate of interest on mortgages and the importance of low-interest rates to the middle-income population. Discussion with a strategic planner centered on the income and savings of the middle-income population. Three experts completed the quantitative questionnaire. Table 1 presents demographic information on the study participants.

Three open-ended qualitative questions prompted participants to share experiences with access to affordable housing. In answering the questions, respondents did not answer other similar questions that fall with the delimiters. There were instances when participants, for reasons beyond the scope of study, decided to not respond to *other questions.*

TABLE 1:
PARTICIPANTS IN THE STUDY

Participant	Age	Gender	Job/Classification
C1	23	Male	CBN Employee
C6	32	Male	CBN Employee
P1	47	Male	Engineer
P2	37	Female	Construction
C2	45	Female	CBN Employee
P3	30	Female	Construction

F2	29	Male	FCDA
F3	43	Male	FCDA
C3	42	Male	CBN Employee
C10	38	Male	CBN Employee
P4	38	Female	Construction
P5	43	Male	Engineer
P6	32	Male	Engineer
F10	42	Male	Construction/ Consultant
C5	45	Female	CBN Employee
C7	32	Male	CBN Employee
C8	45	Male	CBN Employee
C4	26	Male	CBN Employee
C9	38	Male	CBN Employee
F1	47	Male	Engineer
F4	36	Male	Construction
P7	45	Male	Builder
P10	37	Male	Builder
P8	43	Female	Planner
P9	25	Female	Employee
F6	37	Male	Construction
F7	38	Female	Employee
F9	38	Male	CBN Employee
F5	36	Male	Employee
F8	33	Male	Employee
C11	47	Male	Real Estate Expert
P11	37	Male	Expert Planner
F11	35	Male	Financial Expert

At each of the three meetings, participants were welcomed, the purpose of the study was explained, and participants were assured of confidentiality and that participation was voluntary. Participants were purposefully selected within the range of 23 to 47 years old. Selections of participants were purposeful because the average life expectancy of Nigerians was pegged at 48 years and vibrant middle-income earners are those that fall within delimiters (Country Reports, Nigeria 2006). Participants received the qualitative survey first. Once the qualitative survey was returned, participants received the quantitative survey. Participants responded to the quantitative questionnaires with relative ease by circling or checking a particular number (see Appendix A). Quantitative portion of the questionnaire consisted of 25 statements on a 5-point, Likert-type scale with anchors from 1 = *strongly disagree* to 5 = *strongly agree*. A score of 3 indicated a neutral position (see Appendix A).

According to Creswell (2002), Neumann (2003), and Simon (2006), a sample size of not more than 30 is sufficient for a qualitative study. The sample included ten participants from the Central Bank, ten participants from the Federal Capital Development Authority and ten participants from the private sector. Sample size might not reflect the total middle-income population that resides in Abuja. Middle-income populations were nebulously defined as those whose monthly income range from (N10000 to N1250, 000)(S100 to $800 USD) (Country Reports, Nigeria, 2006). Sample size might not be a reflection of additional incentives inculcated into individuals' income range. Other variables such as incentives that might augment income range may have made the participants different from the remaining population of interest. Employees in governmental agencies, the private sector, and financial institutions provided pertinent information regarding the lack of affordable housing in Abuja.

Samples selection from each stratum in Table 2 represented the targeted subgroups within the income range for study. From the targeted subgroups, generalization of the middle-income population capacity to afford housing was depicted. In Abuja, renting a single-family residence cost 8000 to 50000 Naira, the Nigerian currency, and equivalent to $100 to $400 USD (Country Reports, Nigeria, 2006, World Bank Group, 2006). First, the price on housing depends on the location of the property. Second, affordability of housing depends on whether or not two-third of the monthly incomes of the middle-income populations are allocated for housing. Inferably, the sampling of errors confined to study represented an estimation of the middle-income population in Abuja (Ikejiofor, 1998, Neumann, 2003). Table below revealed that housing for the middle-income population remained unaffordable, and thus supported the respondent's qualitative responses.

TABLE 2: *DISPROPORTIONATE STRATIFIED SAMPLING*

Estimated Monthly Income Range of employees (#10000-#75000 =$100-$600)	Estimated General Population Population in Abuja (N)	Volunteer Sample Population	Percent of the Sample Population	Stratified Random Sample	Stratified Sample Percentage	Errors Confine to Population Sample
	7,000,000					
CBN Staff (#25-#125000)	200	130	36.60	30	3.55	+26.4
FCDA Staff (#15000-#45000)	180	120	33.80	30	3.55	+26.4
Private Sector Staff (#10000-#135000)	140	105	29.6	30	3.55	+26.4
Total	520	355	100	90	11.40	+26.4

Note: Sources: Nigerian Central Bank, 2005, Country Reports, Nigeria, 2006: White, 2005

Data Analysis

Three interview questions acted as the instrumentation of study and focused primarily on the research question. Research question guiding study was: how does the lack of affordable housing affect the middle-income population in Abuja? Research process for study began with data analysis from the transcripts of the interviews using modified van Kaam method of analysis by Moustakas (1994). A modified van Kaam method of analysis includes seven steps (p. 121) by Moustakas (1994). Seven steps consisted of the following:

1. Every expression relevant to the experience are listed

2. Each expression are tested for two requirements:

    a. Does the expression contain a moment of the experience that is a necessary and sufficient constituent for understanding the expression?

    b. How possible for the expression to abstract and label the experience? If so, is the expression a horizon of the experience? Any expression not meeting this requirement was eliminated or used in the textural description of the findings.

3. Clustering the invariant constituents to reveal the core themes of the experience.

4. Final identification of the Invariant Constituents and Themes by application.

    a. Explicitly are the constituents expressed?

    b. Are the constituents compatible if not explicitly expressed?

    c. If the invariant constituents are not explicit or compatible then they are not relevant to the phenomenon.

5. How compatible or explicit was the validation of the invariant constituents and themes against the transcriptions.

6. Constructing an individual textural description of each participant's experience (presented in the textural description).

7. Using the themes and invariant constituents to construct a textural-structural description for each participant of the "meanings and essences of the experience" (pp 120-121).

Interviews responses were analyzed for emergent core themes, characteristics, and descriptions using QSR Nvivo7® qualitative data analysis software. Using the software, a systematic discipline to code data in development of themes and definition of common terms was analyzed. Once the data was coded, the program allowed the research process to synthesize data developing clusters or groupings from data. Further synthesis defined data until emergent themes evolved from the invariant constituencies.

For this study, the research assigned a code to the invariant constituencies and stored that data in the QSR Nvivo7® software as directed by the disciplines of the program. For this study, employees from the Central Bank of Nigeria were labeled C1 to C10. For the Federal Capital Development Authority, employees were labeled F1 to F10, and the private sector participants were labeled P1 to P10. Experts were categorized as C11, F11, and P11.

Coding of the participants was used to ground the process. Codes were also used to develop groupings for invariant constituency similarities from the participants' responses to questions in the interview. Using Moustakas (1994) Modified van Kaam method of analysis, or steps one through seven, and the QSR Nvivo7® qualitative data analysis software, the groupings of similar ideals, opinions, or suggestions were identified from the interview transcripts. Next step was to cluster the groupings to develop emergent core themes in relation to the phenomenon.

With comparison during research process, review of the participants' interview transcripts to validate the invariant constituents was analyzed. Individual textural-structural descriptions for each participant's transcript were developed. Composite description based upon the individual textural-structural descriptions and core themes of the data, was developed for the phenomenon (Moustakas). Composite description provides the "meanings and essences of the experience, representing the group as a whole"(Moustakas, p. 121). When the seven steps had been applied, the emergent themes developed; there was a complete process that defined the research study,

Textural descriptions included excerpts of each participant's contribution that was pertinent to the research. Quotes generated from participants during the interview process were explained. Data used in the analysis identify the invariant constituents. Four major core themes were developed from the synthesis of those invariant constituencies. Three interview questions for the study focused on the perceptions and feelings of the middle-income populations that were generated from the primary research question:

1   Based on your experiences, how does the lack of affordable housing affect the middle-income population in Abuja, Nigeria?

2   Based on your experiences, how does the Nigerian culture impact affordable housing and price of housing in Abuja?

3   Based on your experiences, how does technological information exchange between the stakeholders in Abuja result in availability of housing for the middle-income population?

Findings

General Overview

Four major themes emerged from the research data that resulted in the following summarized composite description for this study:

1. *Lack of affordable housing.* Participants stated that housing for middle-income populations are not affordable and there was a lack of affordable housing.

2. *Nigerian culture.* Participants stated that culture did not impact ability of the middle-income population to rent or buy home.

3. *The internet, extranet, and intranet.* The themes emanated from the interview question that asked how does technological information exchange within the stakeholders in Abuja result in availability of housing for the middle-income population? Participants responded to effective communication, exchange of information amongst stakeholders through technology. Finding available housing,

funding of new construction homes and loans to home applicants was pivotal to the method used in disseminating information on housing to the public.

4. *Economic infrastructures:* Participants responded that electricity supply that supports communications was infrequent. Communication linking stakeholders to affordable housing are constantly interrupted. Non-centralization of information on housing within FCDA or the CBN server inhibits finding availability housing. Supply of electricity that supports economic infrastructures remained infrequent as responded to by the participants.

DATA CLUSTERING AND THEMATIZING

The methods and procedures of the phenomenological analysis developed the individual textural-structural descriptions of the participants in this study. Equal weight was given to statements from each participant pertinent to the research study (Moustakas, 1994). Data clustering and thematizing involved grouping the data into core themes that participants revealed during responses (Moustakas). Three interview questions, the data clustering, and thematizing provided empirical evidence supporting the four core themes identified from research study.

1. *Interview question 1: Based on your experiences, does the lack of affordable housing affect the middle-income population in Abuja?* This question was to initiate reaction from participants to the affordability of housing for the middle-income population. Twenty-one participants (70%) responses indicated that housing was not affordable by the middle-income population. Seven participants (30%) responses indicated that housing are available for those who can afford it. All participants agreed that there was a lack of affordable housing affecting the middle-income population.

2. *Interview question 2: Based on your experiences, how does the Nigerian culture impact affordable price of housing in Abuja?* In Nigeria, items are mostly purchased in cash and

conjecturally, owning a home in Abuja means paying cash (Ibagere, 2002). Because of the cultural motifs attached to institutional loans, this question was pertinent to understanding how participants view financial institutions, or detach institutional loans from the Nigerian culture. Twenty-eight participants (85%) responses indicated that culture has no impact on the price of housing. Two participants (15%) indicated that Nigerian culture could inhibit how middle-income population view institutional loans; culture has no direct effect with availability of affordable housing for the middle-income population.

3. *Interview question three: Based on your experiences, how does technological information exchange between the stakeholders in Abuja result in availability of housing for the middle-income population?* Globally, technology information and the use of technology to transact businesses in real estate are concurrently adopted (Drucker & Peters, 2002). Suggestively, the purpose of the question was to find out how effective and helpful was the used of technology amongst stakeholders in the enhancement of housing transactions for the targeted population segment. Twenty-four participants (80%) who responded to this question agreed that exchange of information amongst the stakeholders would result in availability of information regarding housing loans or leases to the target population. Six participants (20%) responded that technology exchange between stakeholders would not change the price of housing.

4. *Other qualitative and quantitative questions.* Other qualitative and quantitative questions within the delimiters were purposefully asked to help support and complement the three core interview questions. Interview questions and survey questionnaires that fall within the delimiters were asked as a supportive role to the three core interview questions.

QUALITATIVE DATA

Interview Question 1: Based on your experiences, how does the lack of affordable housing affect the middle-income population in Abuja, Nigeria?

1. C1 (CBN Employee): "Housing are expensive and the middle-income earners cannot afford housing accommodation."

2. C2, CBN Employee: "Housing accommodation is affordable if you have the means. Within my income range, I cannot afford to buy any house, I can only rent in towns like Wusa, Asokoro, and Matama, however, depends on the amount the landlord demand for rent."

3. C3: "middle income population cannot afford housing in the central area of the city."

4. C4: "Housing is not affordable due to the income of the middle-income population."

5. C5: "Housing shortage affects middle-income population due to their income range."

6. C6: "I will describe the effect of a lack of affordable housing if one third of my income cannot be used to pay for rent, or buy a house. If one third of my income cannot meet this test, housing is not affordable as far as I am concerned."

7. C7: "Sure, housing are not affordable to the average person in Abuja." I think Abuja is designed for only the rich people or people who can afford housing."

8. C8: "I don't think housing are affordable in Abuja. Middle-income population, like myself, are finding it difficult to maintained housing with our income and extended family members to support."

9. C9: "Accommodation in Abuja is not affordable if you are making an average of N50000 or less."

10. C10: "I think the mortgage banks should step to help defray the burden of affordable housing affecting the middle-income population."

1. P1 (Private Sector Employee): "Housing is affordable, it all depends on where you want to stay or live. Housing is affordable if you manage your income properly.'

2. P2: "Housing is not affordable in Abuja if you are a middle-income earners. It is better you go and live in the satellite towns, such as Kubwa, Yahaya, Gwagwalada and other suburban areas in Abuja."

3. P3: "I think the government design Abuja to eliminate housing for the middle-income population. Why is it that only people with higher income of say six figures can afford housing in the cities within Abuja? For example, in Gwaripa, renting a three bedroom apartment cost N50, 000 a month, not talking about the most expensive areas of the cities such as Asokoro, or Matana, and Wusa areas where the rent on housing doubles. Tell me how an average income earners can afford housing of this nature."

4. P4: "I do not believe affordable housing is the issue. In my opinion and experience, income, cost of living, and other microeconomic issues arc factors leading to the lack of affordable housing."

5. P5: "I will describe affordable housing as housing that are within the reach of what individuals are willing to pay for it and stay in the house."

6. P6: "Housing for the middle-income population is expensive and not affordable, and this affect people with my income."

7. P7: "… My take on this question is that Abuja housing for the middle-income population does not exists."

8. P8: "I feel Affordable housing for the middle income population could be achievable if the interest rates attached to loans are not that high. Even the down payments required by financial institution are 25% to 50%. I cannot afford that. Maybe a reduction of down payment could help middle-income population capacity to afford housing, and this affect my lifestyle."

9. P9: "My opinion is that highly priced housing affect the middle-income populations who cannot afford housing in Abuja."

10. P10: "My understanding of this question is that housing or accommodation are expensive and a lack of affordable housing impact the standard of living of people like me (the middle-income earners)."

1. F1 (FCDA Employee): "…. In my view, the lack of affordable housing is very subjective, depending on whether or not you can afford it or not. To middle-income earners, the effects of the lack of housing affect their levels of production and capacity to perform at an optimal."

2. F2: "… Yes, I feel middle-income populations are affected by the lack of affordable housing due to their income range. For me, housing in Abuja eats up two third of my income which is not good. I cannot afford to live in a decent place because of the price attached to housing."

3. F3: "I think the effects of lack of affordable housing on middle-income population are due to governmental housing policies. Housing policies for the middle-income population are not properly implemented to benefit those affected. Housings are mostly regarded to be for only the rich in Abuja."

4. F4: "…Come on, in my opinion, there are no middle-income people in Abuja, so, affordable housing cannot affect them."

5. F5: "You have to live in Abuja for you to have thorough impact of the effect of affordable housing and how it affect people like me. Low-income, higher interest rates, higher down payments, paying rent one or two years in advance are factors embedded in the housing market that affect people like me-the middle-income population."

6. F6: "In my experience as a middle-income earners the lack of affordable housing is due to the overwhelming amount of

money required to rent an accommodation or buy a home in Abuja."

7. F7: "… Yes, with my five experience of living in Abuja, housing is available for the middle-income people who can afford it. If one can afford housing, it limits the amount of negative effect or impact into my lifestyle."

8. F8: "To me, most importantly apart from food is shelter. If shelter is not affordable, there goes the total economy of a nation. It is paramount that housing should be affordable to people like me (the middle-income population) because we are at the core of a nation's development."

9. F9: "I do not believe housing affect the middle-income population. Affordable housing is subjective and depends how a person dissect it. If you can afford housing, you are not affected, but if you cannot afford housing you are affected."

10. F10: "Affordable is relevant to people like me-middle-income population and should be addressed by the city or housing policy makers."

Interview Question 2: Based on your experiences, how does the Nigerian culture impact affordable housing and price of housing in Abuja?

1. CI (CBN Employee): " With my five years experience in looking for affordable housing in Abuja, culture has no impact on the price of housing."

2. C2: "Nigerian culture is both individualistic and collectivistic, and I am not sure in my experience of finding available housing for rent how this has impacted the price of housing in Abuja."

3. C3: "I think culture has more to do with affordable housing because people sometimes are not comfortable culturally accepting loans to build their homes."

4. C4: "Culture in Nigerian is divergent and people interpret it to mean different things to them and may or may not have

an impact on the price of housing. To me, culture has no bearing on the price of housing."

5. C5: "I think, Nigerian culture dictates to some degree that cash should be used to rent, or buy property, and this factor may affect affordable housing."

6. C6: "Invariably, I think of culture as the way people do things. Nigerian has over 250 cultural elements or dialects. Generally, these elements within the culture, I feel have effects on the price of housing."

7. C7: "I do not see any correlation between culture, price, and affordable housing."

8. C8: "Nigerian culture may have some effect on how people view institutional loans. Nigeria, culturally, is a cash oriented society and this may have impact on the price of housing. My experience of finding an accommodation or the price on housing has nothing to do with my culture."

9. C9: "I will say categorically, that culture has nothing to do housing or price of housing."

10. C10: "Nigerian culture, I feel affects the mentality of people like me to be thinking subliminally that culture dictates the price of housing."

1. P1 (Private Sector Employee): " Culture has no direct impact to the price of affordable housing or how a lack of affordable housing affect the middle-income population in Abuja."

2. P2: "Nigerian culture may affect the ability of people like me- middle-income people to effectively rent or buy a home in Abuja due to how we may view avenues of accepting loans or method of paying for housing. However, I do not think culture by itself has anything to do with a lack of affordable housing. I feel that those middle-income people who can afford housing will afford it anyway regardless of what culture they subscribe to."

3. P3: "In my experience of finding accommodation in Abuja, culture is irrelevant when it comes to the price of housing

whether or not the middle-income population can afford housing."

4. P4: "I do not see any relationship with the Nigerian culture and housing.

5. P5: "Nigerian culture allows individuals to view banks loans differently. My assumption or belief is that people who historically use banks loans to construct personal residences are regarded as financially not buoyant. But today, that is not the case; banks are willing to give loans for construction of personal residency if the collateral is there. These actions may affect affordable housing in Abuja."

6. P6: "Nigerian culture in my opinion has no effect on affordable housing or the lack of affordable housing by the middle-income population."

7. P7: "Culture and housing, in my experience of finding accommodation in Abuja are not related. However, your tribe may affect the decision of the landlord to rent a place to you. But, I think ultimately money talks. If you have money to rent a place, the landlord has no option but to give it to you."

8. P8: "Nigerian Culture in my experience of seeking homes in Abuja for five years has no impact on housing."

9. P9: " … Now, I do not see how culture affects housing for the middle-income population.

10. P10. "Housing is expensive in Abuja, but Nigerian culture is not the cause of expensive houses."

1. F1 (FCDA Employee): "I do not see culture as part of the housing shortage, predicaments facing the middle-income population or part of the reasons of a lack of affordable housing exists."

2. F2: "I see culture to be totally different and irrelevant to the issues of a lack of affordable housing affecting the middle-income populations in Abuja."

3. F3: "My experience in finding accommodation in Abuja for the past six years has no direct impact to my culture."

4. F4: "In my experience and opinion, culture should be separate from the housing."

5. F5: "Housing and culture do not mix. In my view, the discussion regarding the lack of affordable housing affecting middle-income population should be separated."

6. F6: "My experience in seeking accommodation in Abuja in the past six months rests on solely on my ability to pay which as nothing to do with my culture."

7. F7: "I cannot understand when people are unable to pay for housing, they then blame it on culture. Nigerian culture does not build homes or finance loans for homes."

8. F8: "Nigerian culture to me has nothing to do housing."

9. F9: "I do not see the relevant of the Nigerian culture to housing."

10. F10: "My experience in Abuja for the past nine years tells me that culture, affordable housing or the lack of affordable are separate subjects."

Interview Question 3: Based on your experiences, how does technological information exchange between stakeholders in Abuja result in availability of housing for the middle-income population?

1. C1 (CBN Employee): "In my opinion, the importance of technology to the stakeholders in housing cannot be under-estimated. Technology… specifically, the internet will help middle –income population to find available housing."

2. C2: "Effective technology communication means housing for the middle-income people can easily be accessed. Technology will not lead to price reduction in my opinion and experience of finding available housing in Abuja."

3. C3: "My take on this question is that technology could lead to efficiency of finding available housing in Abuja. Financial institutions could use a centralized server to disseminate

information on potential loan applicants amongst the middle-income people."

4. C4: "Financial institution, the governmental agencies, and the private sector could communicate effectively and efficiently through the use of technology. In my difficult experience in locating affordable housing, I think communication that are effectively disseminated on housing will lead to location of available housing."

5. C5: "In my opinion, does people care about technology? Technology only supplements other available information on housing. If housing is not available, technology will not bring available housing to the people."

6. C6: "My take on technology is that without proper economic infrastructure, technology cannot function to bring available housing to the people who really need the information."

7. C7: "I see technology as the only way to effectively transact buying and selling of housing to the middle-income people. Technology will create other available information on potential loan applicants in the process of buying and selling of homes."

8. C8: "I candidly believed that technology-the internet, extranet, and intranet is here to stay. Abuja housing system should be integrated into the technological system. Housing will become available on a global scale. People can log into system and find housing that they so desire."

9. C9: "Technology will allow stakeholders to communicate internal and external. Internally, in my opinion, mean stakeholders sharing pertinent information on housing with each entity. Externally, means sharing the information with the middle-income people."

10. C10: "My question to this question is that if there is infrequent supply of electricity, how can technology be useful to finding available housing for the people like me-middle-income population. It will be difficult."

1. P1 (Private Sector Employee): What I see in today's economy is strong present of technological information in all business. Therefore, technological information on housing will lead to availability of housing for the middle-income people."

2. P1: "I see information exchange within the stakeholders to be the panacea to finding available housing. Exchange of information will lead to other aspect of producing efficient housing programs for the middle-income population. "

3. P3: "In my experience, the internet will help me locate available housing for lease or buy in Abuja, that is if the information is available."

4. P4: "I think available information on where to get low-interest loans, available housing or governmental grants for housing is necessary. The key issue will be how the stakeholders coordinate this information and make available to the middle-income people that needs it."

5. P5: "Information technological remained important to finding available housing in my opinion and experience in finding reasonable accommodation."

6. P6: "My experience in finding an accommodation with my income has been difficult due to lack of information coming from either the financial institutions, real estate managers, or through governmental agencies."

7. P7: "I feel that information are intentional provided in piece meal or made scarce due to fact that people with the information are beneficiary of the scarcity of the information. I think, people like me-middle-income earners will continue to experience hardship when it comes to available information on housing."

8. P8: "In my opinion, the good thing about technological exchange amongst the stakeholders is that it would force them to create a centralized server to monitor housing information. But, I wonder whether or not they will

exchange information for the benefit of the middle-income earners or will the *status quo* remain."

9. P9: "In Abuja, you have to think twice if you think information technology within the stakeholders will result in available housing for the middle-income population. The problem, in my experience for the past five years, housing for the middle-income earners are not available."

10. P10: "In my experience in living in Abuja for the past seven years, technological exchange of information will only occur when there are proper economic infrastructures. For example, the supply of electricity is infrequent, supply of basic amenities like water is not available. In my opinion, these amenities will help support information technology."

1. F1 (FCDA Employee): "In my office, we have access to the internet. Placing available information on the internet by the stakeholders on how potential loan applicants can find loans and housings, obtain low-interest rate loans, and information on the subject properties will be useful."

2. F2: "Exchange of technological information on housing in my experience will expedite finding available housing, expedite loan processing time, and expedite sharing of information amongst the stakeholders which is to their benefit."

3. F3: "The stakeholders in my experience are benefiting from the present housing shortages or housing bottle necks, if not, why would they want change anything. Information exchange on housing will help middle-income earners find available housing, but will not "reduce the cost or price on housing."

4. F4: "In my experience housing and available information on housing are critical to locating housing are available within the city. Economic infrastructure such as roads, water, and supply of electricity to locating properties are equally important. Stakeholders should provide information in a centralized database to enable potential home finders to

make a choice. Having a choice in where one lives makes a big difference."

5. F5: "Whether or not stakeholders exchange information is irrelevant in my experience when it comes to finding available housing. To economic factors such as one's income and cost of living makes the information useful. In my opinion is one thing to get information, another thing is to make use of the information successfully."

6. F6: "In my experience information exchange within stakeholders could create a data mine, that will benefit the stakeholders."

7. F7: "In my experience technological exchange within stakeholders is good for the middle-income people, because information on available homes would be easy to find, fund, and sold in the open market."

8. F8: "In my experience, housing available should be shared within the stakeholders who will equally share the information to the public and particularly to the middle-income people who need reasonable accommodation, and where it could be found."

9. F9: "In my experience information exchange by the stakeholders will not make any difference to the finding available housing for the middle-income population, because they cannot afford houses in Abuja main town anyway."

10. F10: " ...Yes, in my experience, exchange of information on housing in a technological peripherals or the internet will help stakeholder shown where available housing are plausible for people like me."

OTHER INTERVIEW QUESTIONS

Interview Question 4. How do you feel about housing availability and affordability for the middle-income population?

Data suggested that the middle-income population was unable to afford reasonable accommodation based on the current salary range. Participant F5 (FCDA Engineer) stated that "the income or salary for housing was not enough." Participant F2 (Builder) responded to the same question by stating that "the middle-income earners are

not welcome in Abuja due to the price attached to housing"(see Appendix E).

Interview Question 5: How would you describe financial institutions' capacity to establish low-interest construction and mortgage loans to middle-income earners in Abuja?

Participants responded that financial institutions have the capacity to establish low-interest construction and mortgage loans to middle-income earners. Current loans available to the middle-income earners are over 10%. Participant F3 (FCDA Staff) stated that "financial institutions are doing nothing for the middle-income earners except for their friends, and the interest rates on loans are high." Participants P7, P8, P5, F8, F9, F10, F3, P6, and P10 agreed with the assertion. Participants' responses indicated that loans are available to the middle-income population, but at a double-digit interest rate.

Interview Question 6: How would you describe the private sector in relation to affordable housing?

Participants P6, P2, F6, F7, F8, C3, C6, C7, C8, P7, and P8 revealed that the private sector should build houses to complement governmental efforts in reducing housing. Participant F3 (FCDA Staff) stated that "there was no good governmental policy yet in place for housing."

Interview Question 7: How does communication in your organization improve housing availability or lead to affordability of housing for the middle-income population?

Participants P8, P2, P10, F8, F9, F10, C8, C9, C10, and P9 indicated that communication improved housing availability due to the present internet and telecommunication infrastructures in the city. Individuals emphasized that information on availability of houses was disseminated through the traditional methods. Participant P10, a real estate consultant for 13 years, stated that "real estate agents who engaged in housing transactions move from [one] area of the city to another while locating available housing." There was no specialized center or centralized computerized server that provides information on housing data. According to Participant P2 (Builder/Developer), "technology has not been fully developed for housing transactions in Abuja."

Interview Question 8: How will an electronic marketplace provide information on housing to the middle-income population?

Participants P1, P2, P3, F1, F2, F3, C1, C2, and C3 indicated that the internet cafes or centers are available within reach of the middle-income population; the internet cafes are sparsely spread within the city. Participant F2 (FCDA Staff) stated that the "internet will provide good information on housing but will not provide substantive information on affordability housing in Abuja"(see Appendix E). The synopsis was that the internet does not help create housing or help provide accommodation for the middle-income population.

Interview Question 9: How would you describe the effect of culture on governmental housing policies?

There was no consensus in the responses to question seven. Participants P4, P5, P6, F4, F5, and F6 indicated that culture was individualistic based on ethnicity or language, and has "no relationship with housing" (Participant P5, Engineer and Consultant). By contrast, Participants C4, C5 C6, P4, P5, and P6 indicated that the Nigerian culture was collectivistic, depending on what tribe a person or group of people comes from. Participant P5 stated that within the 253 mixed ethnicities and languages, "culture has no impact on housing."

Interview Question 10: How would you describe culture with respect to housing within the private sector?

Data from Participants P7, P8, P9, F7, F8, and F9 suggested that the culture of people shaped how individuals interpret the difficulties associated with finding reasonable accommodations. Participant P2, a real estate developer for ten years, indicated that "culture has nothing to do one's ability to buy or lease reasonable accommodation in Abuja. That finding reasonable accommodation should not be affront to the dignity of the middle-income population. According to C10, "seller prices or loans attached to houses available for lease or buy are subjective and has no cultural impact on the housing market"(Participant C10, Real Estate Management Consultant).

Interview Question 11: How would you describe partnerships and stakeholders in the housing market?

The data from Participants C3, P7, P8, P5, F8, F9, F10, C8, C9, P6, and P10 indicated that positive relationships existed between the stakeholders. The existence of positive stakeholder relationships does not translate into providing housing for the middle-income earners in the form of a social program. According to Participant C3 (CBN Executive), "Profit making was the ultimate goal of the stakeholders."

Interview Question 12: What is your experience with housing accommodation in Abuja?

Participants C1, P9, P8, F10, F9, F8, C10, C9, C8, and P10 indicated that housing was available and relatively expensive for the middle-income population. "Finding reasonable accommodation could take up to six months, depending on the location or area of the city where homes are available"(Participant C1, CBN Employee).

QUANTITATIVE DATA

For this study, the second step was a survey questionnaire consisted of 25 statements on a 5-point Likert-type scale with anchors from *strongly agree* to *strongly disagree*. Statements on the questionnaire were formulated using information from the literature reviewed. Statements included most pertinent variables in the topic of lack of affordable housing in Abuja as described in Chapter 2. Statistical analyses below are used to support the inductive responds and perspectives of the middle-income populations.

Age and gender. Respondents ranged in age from 23 to 47, with a mean of 36.63, a median of 37.5 and mode of 38, and a standard deviation of 7.33. Of the 30 respondents, 22 (73.3%) were male and eight (26.7%) were female (see Figure 3).

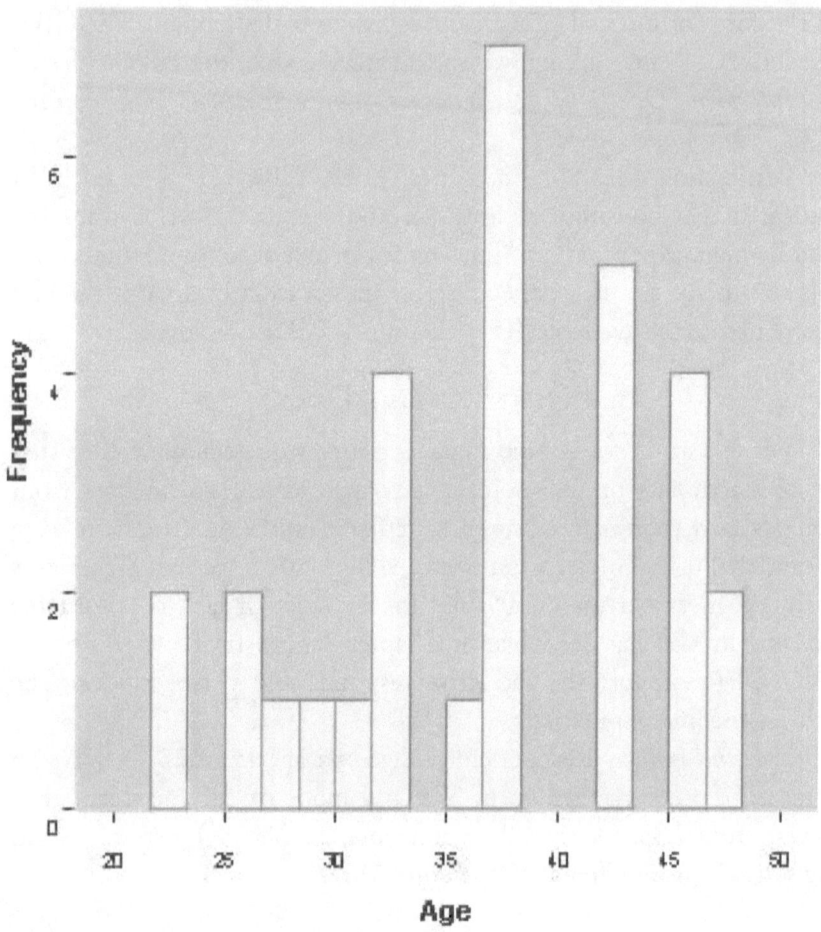

Figure 3. Participant age

Survey results. Quantitative portion of the questionnaire consisted of 25 statements on a 5-point Likert-type scale with anchors from 1 = *strongly disagree* to 5 = *strongly agree.* A score of three indicated a neutral position (see Appendix A). Survey question one asked respondents whether or not affordable *housing is core to a nation's development.* Nine respondents (30%) agreed with the statement and 21 (70%) strongly agreed with the statement.

Question one had a mean of 4.7, a mode of 5, and a standard deviation of .46, indicating that the all the respondents agreed or strongly agreed that affordable housing was core to a nation's development (see Figure

4). In comparison, the three experts all strongly agreed that affordable housing was core to a nation's development.

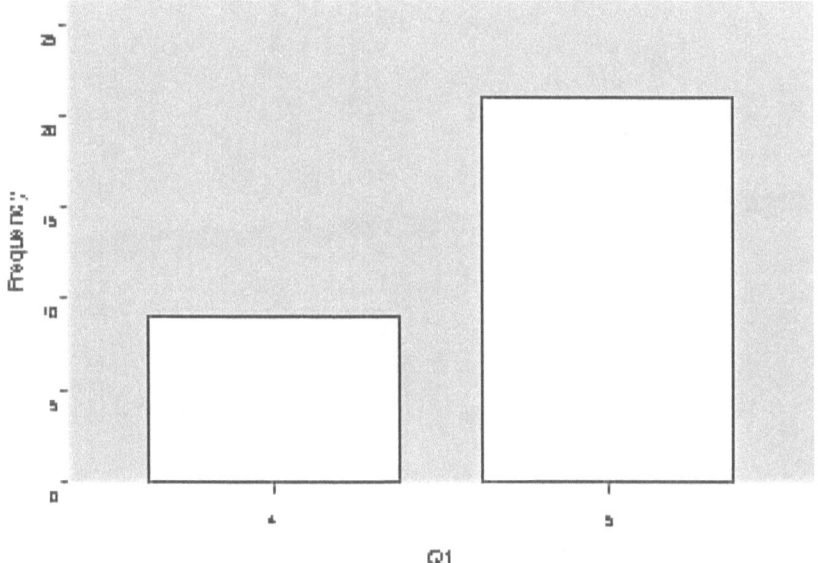

Figure 4. Question 1-Bar grap
4=Agree, 5=Strongly Agree.

Bar graph – question one asked if *affordable housing was core to a nation's development.* For the larger portion of the bar graph represented participant's who agreed or strongly agreed that affordable housing was core to a nation's development. Smaller portion of the bar graph represented participants who disagree with the survey question.

Survey question two asked respondents if *affordable housing to the middle-income population is part of a nation's infrastructure.* Eleven respondents (36.7%) agreed with the statement, and 19 (63.3%) strongly agreed with the statement. Question two had a mean of 4.63, a mode of 5, and a standard deviation of .49, indicating that the majority agreed or strongly agreed that affordable housing to the middle-income population was part of a nation's infrastructure (see Figure 5).

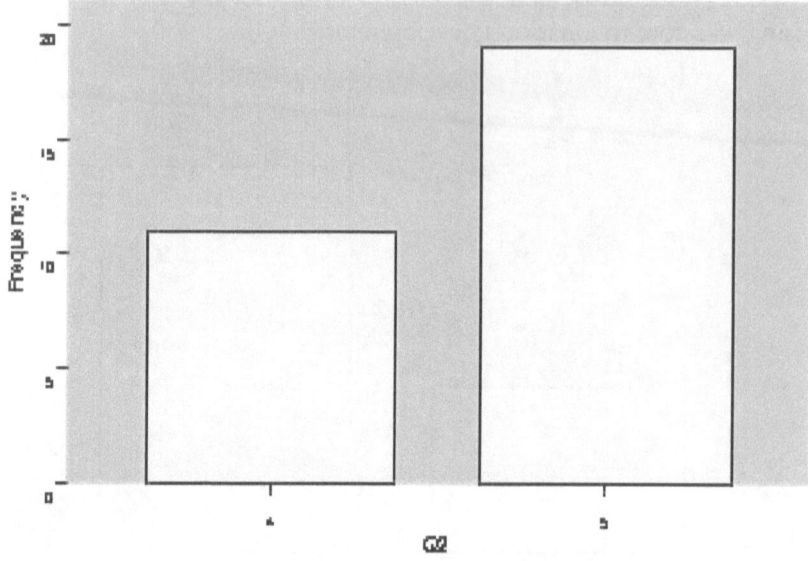

Figure 5. Question 2-Bar graph
4=Agree, 5=Strongly Agree.

Bar graph – question two asked respondents if *affordable housing to the middle-income population is part of a nation's infrastructure.* As represented in the bar graph, eleven respondents (36.7%) agreed with the statement, and 19 (63.3%) strongly agreed with the statement. Represented in the smaller bar are the portion of participates that did not agree with the survey question. In comparison, the experts had a mean of 4.33, a mode of 4.0, and a standard deviation of .58, agreeing with the respondents.

Survey question three asked respondents whether or not *affordable housing does not affect me.* Two respondents (6.7%) strongly disagreed, two respondents (6.7%) disagreed, four respondents (13.3%) were neutral, 13 respondents (43.3%) agreed, and nine respondents (30%) strongly agreed. Question three had a mean of 3.83, a mode of 4, and a standard deviation of 1.15, indicating a lack of agreement that affordable housing does not affect the individual (see Figure 6).

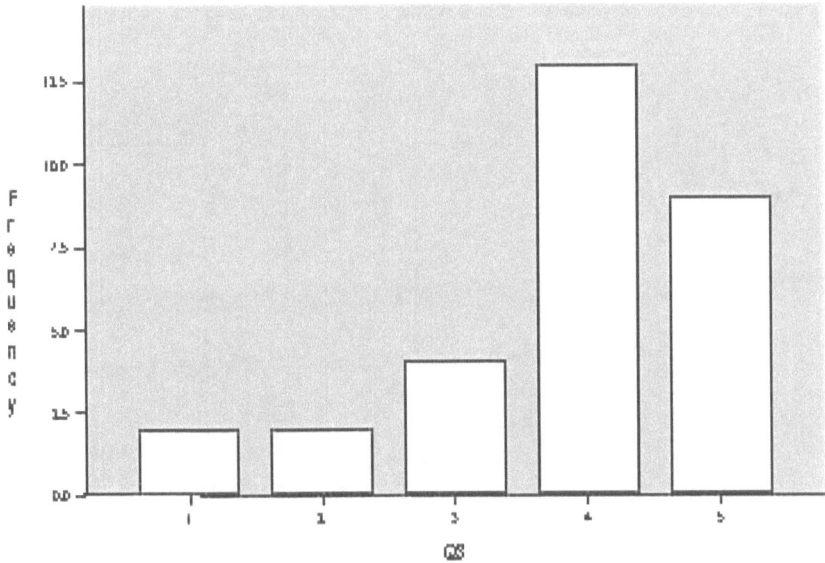

Figure 6. Question 3-Bar graph
1=Strongly Disagree to 5=Strongly Agree.

Bar graph –question three asked respondents whether or not *affordable housing does not affect me.* Indicated in the bar graph, two respondents (6.7%) strongly disagreed, two respondents (6.7%) disagreed, four respondents (13.3%) were neutral, 13 respondents (43.3%) agreed, and nine respondents (30%) strongly agreed. Explained in the bar graph is that affordable housing affected majority of the participants. All three experts were neutral.

Survey question four asked respondents if housing *is subsidized through my employer.* One respondent (3.3%) disagreed, nine respondents (30%) were neutral, 11 respondents (36.7%) agreed, and nine respondents (30%) strongly agreed. Question four had a mean of 3.93, a mode of 4, and a standard deviation of .87, indicating a lack of agreement that housing was subsidized by employers, though the trend was slightly more in agreement than for question three (see Figure 7).

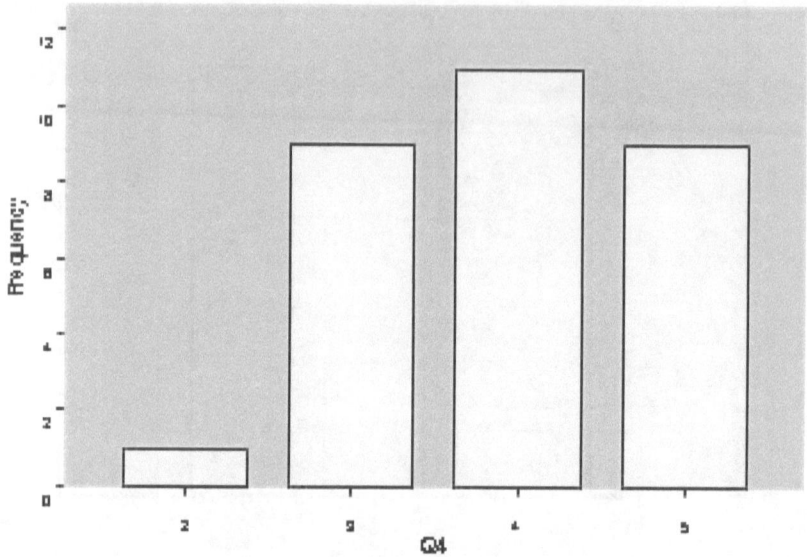

Figure 7. Question 4-Bar graph
2= Disagree to 5 = Strongly Agree.

Bar graph – question four asked respondents if housing *was subsidized through my employer.* Indicated in the bar graph, one respondent (3.3%) disagreed, nine respondents (30%) were neutral, 11 respondents (36.7%) agreed, and nine respondents (30%) strongly agreed. Participants in the bar graph were neutral and in agreement with the survey question. All three experts strongly disagreed.

Survey question five asked respondents if *there are no middle-income earners in Abuja.* One respondent (3.3%) strongly disagreed, four respondents (13.3%) disagreed, 14 respondents (46.7%) were neutral, seven respondents (23.3%) agreed, and four respondents (13.3%) strongly agreed. Question 5 had a mean of 3.3, a mode of 4, and a standard deviation of .99, indicating a lack of agreement that middle-income earners in Abuja do not exist (see Figure 8).

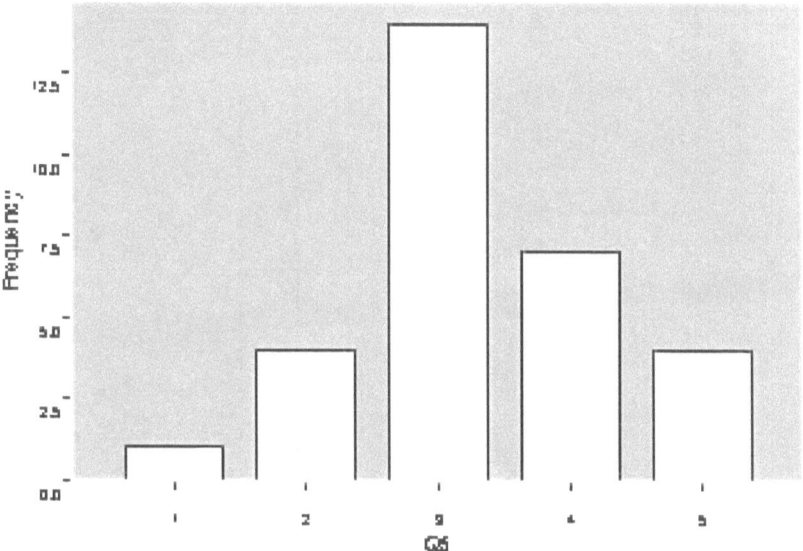

Figure 8. Question 5-Bar graph
1=Strongly Disagree to 5=Strongly Agree.

Bar graph –question five asked respondents if *there are no middle-income earners in Abuja.* Showed in the bar graph, one respondent (3.3%) strongly disagreed, four respondents (13.3%) disagreed, 14 respondents (46.7%) were neutral, seven respondents (23.3%) agreed, and four respondents (13.3%) strongly agreed. Neutrality that emanated from the bar graph indicated participants were not sure whether or not middle-income earners could afford housing. All three experts agreed there are no middle-income earners in Abuja.

Survey question six asked respondents whether or not *only the rich can afford housing.* No participants strongly disagreed, seven respondents (23.3%) disagreed, 11 respondents (36.7%) were neutral, 12 respondents (40%) agreed, and no respondents strongly agreed. Question six had a mean of 3.17, a mode of 4, and a standard deviation of .79, indicating a slight trend toward agreement that only the rich can afford housing (see Figure 9).

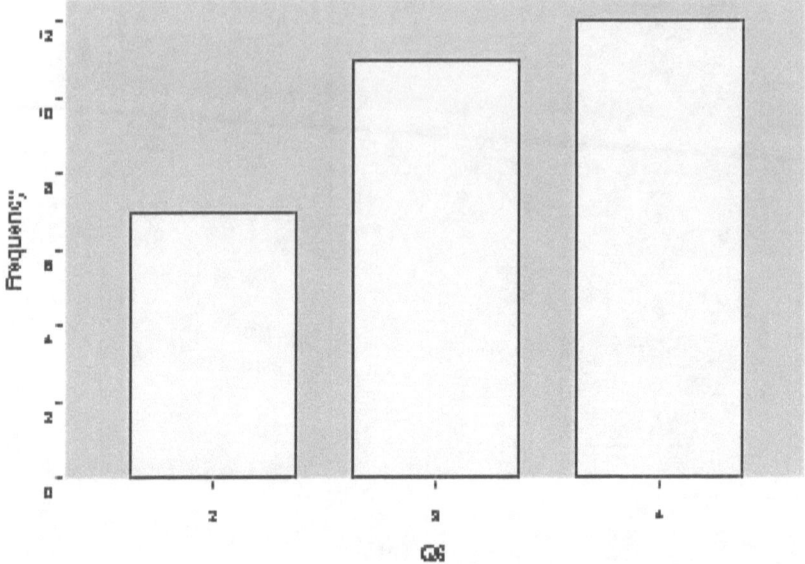

Figure 9. Question 6-Bar graph
2=Disagree, 3=Neutral, 4=Agree.

Bar graph –question six asked respondents whether or not *only the rich could afford housing.* No participants in the bar graph strongly disagreed, seven respondents (23.3%) disagreed, 11 respondents (36.7%) were neutral, 12 respondents (40%) agreed, and no respondents strongly agreed. Explained in the bar graph that only the rich could afford housing. One expert was neutral and two experts agreed with survey question six.

Survey question seven asked respondents whether or not *without low-interest loans, there would be no affordable housing.* Two respondents (6.7%) strongly disagreed, two respondents (6.7%) disagreed, ten respondents (33.3%) were neutral, eight respondents (26.7%) agreed, and eight respondents (26.7%) strongly agreed. Question seven had a mean of 3.6; a mode of 3, and a standard deviation of 1.16, indicating a lack of agreement whether or not without low-interest loans, there will be no affordable housing (see Figure 10).

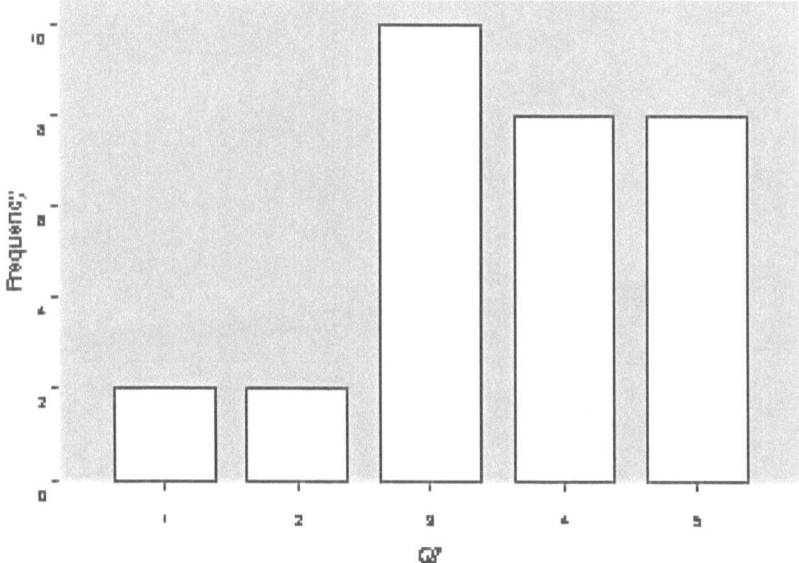

Figure 10. Question 7-Bar graph
1=Strongly Disagree to 5=Strongly Agree.

Bar graph – question seven asked respondents whether or not *without low-interest loans, there would be no affordable housing.* Two respondents as showed in the bar graph (6.7%) strongly disagreed, two respondents (6.7%) disagreed, ten respondents (33.3%) were neutral, eight respondents (26.7%) agreed, and eight respondents (26.7%) strongly agreed. Indicated in the bar graph is neutrality and agreement to the survey question. Neutrality that emerged from bar graph indicated that participants are not sure whether or not low-interest loans could lead to affordable housing. Two experts agreed, and one expert strongly agreed that without low-interest loans, there would be no affordable housing.

Survey question eight asked respondents if *there was a housing shortage.* One respondent (3.3%) strongly disagreed, five respondents (16.7%) disagreed, 12 respondents (40%) were neutral, nine respondents (30%) agreed, and three respondents (10%) strongly agreed. Question eight had a mean of 3.27, a mode of 3, and a standard deviation of .98, indicating participants tended to slightly agree that there was a housing shortage (see Figure 11).

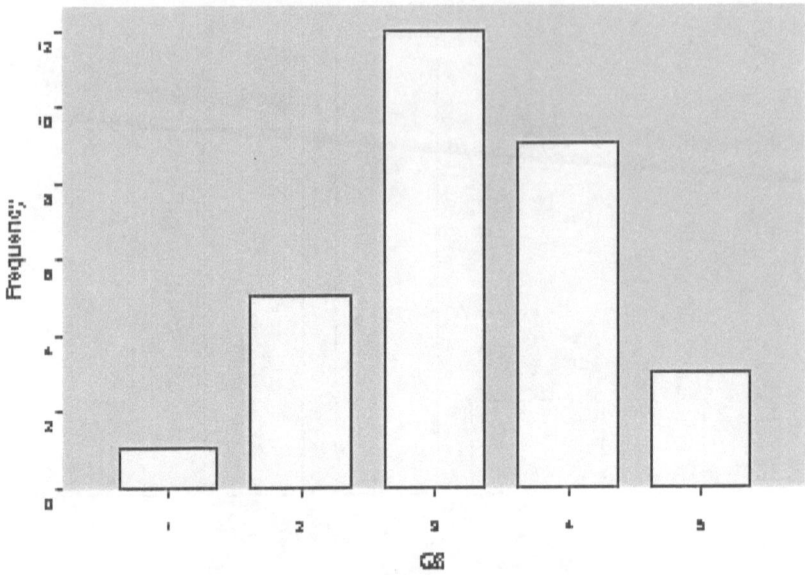

Figure 11. Question 8-Bar graph
1=Strongly Disagree to 5=Strongly Agree.

Bar graph – question eight asked respondents if *there was a housing shortage.* One respondent (3.3%) strongly disagreed, five respondents (16.7%) disagreed, 12 respondents (40%) were neutral, nine respondents (30%) agreed, and three respondents (10%) strongly agreed. Neutrality that emerged from the bar graph indicated that participants were not sure if housing shortage exists in Abuja. All three experts agreed there was a housing shortage.

Survey question nine asked respondents if *housing accommodations are available.* Two (6.7%) strongly disagreed, five respondents (16.7%) disagreed, nine respondents (30%) were neutral, 11 respondents (36.7%) agreed, and three respondents (10%) strongly agreed. Question nine had a mean of 3.27, a mode of 4, and a standard deviation of 1.08, indicating participants tended to slightly agree that housing accommodations are available (see Figure 12).

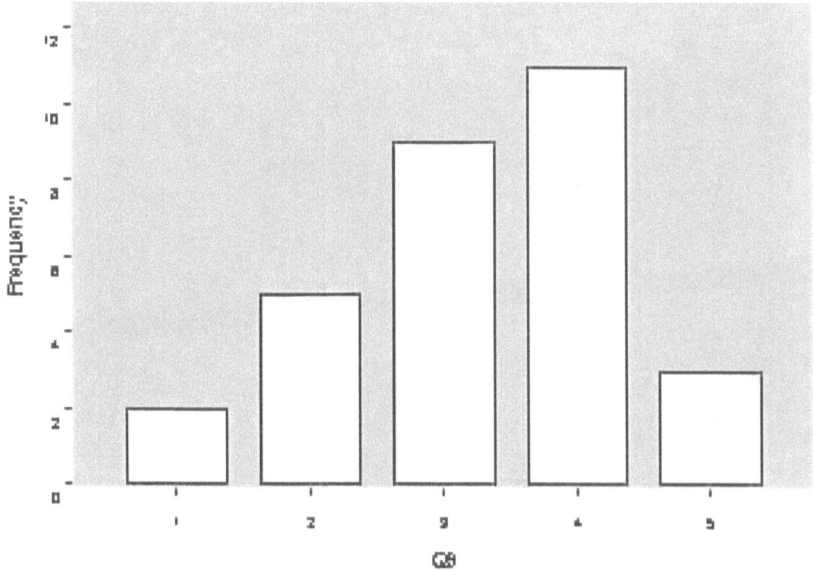

Figure 12. Question 9-Bar graph
1=Strongly Disagree to 5=Strongly Agree.

Bar graph – question nine asked respondents if *housing accommodations are available.* Indicated in the bar graph, two respondents (6.7%) strongly disagreed, five respondents (16.7%) disagreed, nine respondents (30%) were neutral, 11 respondents (36.7%) agreed, and three respondents (10%) strongly agreed. Explained in the bar graph an agreement amongst the participants that housing accommodations were available. Two experts were neutral and one expert strongly agreed that housing accommodations are available.

Survey question ten asked respondents whether or not *the internet was important to affordable housing.* Six respondents (20%) strongly disagreed, six respondents (20%) disagreed, five respondents (16.7%) were neutral, four respondents (13.3%) agreed, and nine respondents (30%) strongly agreed. Question ten had a mean of 3.13, a mode of 5, and a standard deviation of 1.55, indicating little agreement whether or not the internet was important to affordable housing (see Figure 13).

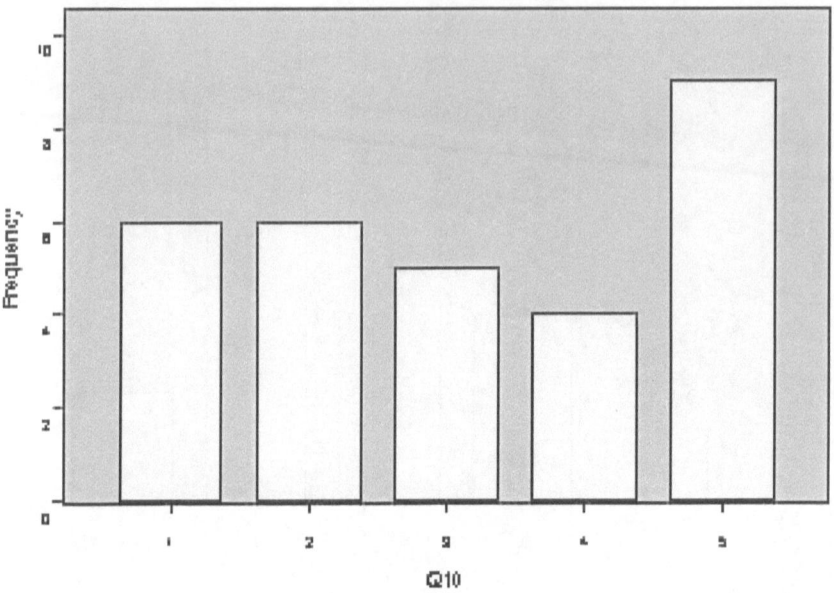

Figure 13. Question 10-Bar graph
1 = Strongly Disagree to 5 = Strongly Agree.

Bar graph – question ten asked respondents whether or not *the internet was important to affordable housing.* Represented in the bar graph (20%) participants that strongly disagreed, (20%) disagreed, (16.7%) neutral, (13.3%) agreed, and (30%) strongly agreed. Overall, the bar graph indicated that the internet remained important to finding affordable housing. One expert agreed and two experts strongly agreed with survey question ten.

Survey question 11 asked respondents if *communication was vital to affordable housing.* One respondent (3.3%) strongly disagreed, one respondent (3.3%) disagreed, eight respondents (26.7%) were neutral, 14 respondents (46.7%) agreed, and six respondents (20%) strongly agreed. Question 11 had a mean of 3.77; a mode of 4, and a standard deviation of .94, indicating participants tended to agree that communication remained vital to affordable housing (see Figure 14).

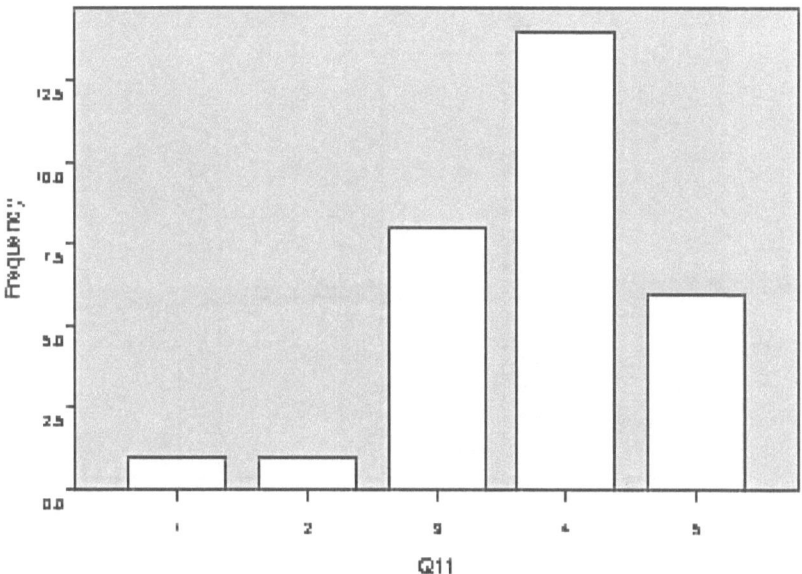

Figure 14. Question 11-Bar graph
1 = Strongly Disagree to 5 = Strongly Agree.

Bar graph – question 11 asked respondents if *communication was vital to affordable housing.* Indicated in the bar graph (3.3%) participants strongly disagreed, (3.3%) disagreed, (26.7%) were neutral, (46.7%) agreed and (20%) strongly agreed. Participants showed in the bar graph are in agreement to why communication remained vital to affordable housing. One expert was neutral and two experts strongly agreed with survey question 11.

Survey question 12 asked respondents whether or not *culture affects affordable housing.* No respondents strongly disagreed, five respondents (16.7%) disagreed, 13 respondents (43.3%) were neutral, eight respondents (26.7%) agreed, and four respondents (13.3%) strongly agreed. Question 12 had a mean of 3.37; a mode of 4, and a standard deviation of 1.09, indicating participants were neutral or tended to agree that culture affect affordable housing (see Figure 15).

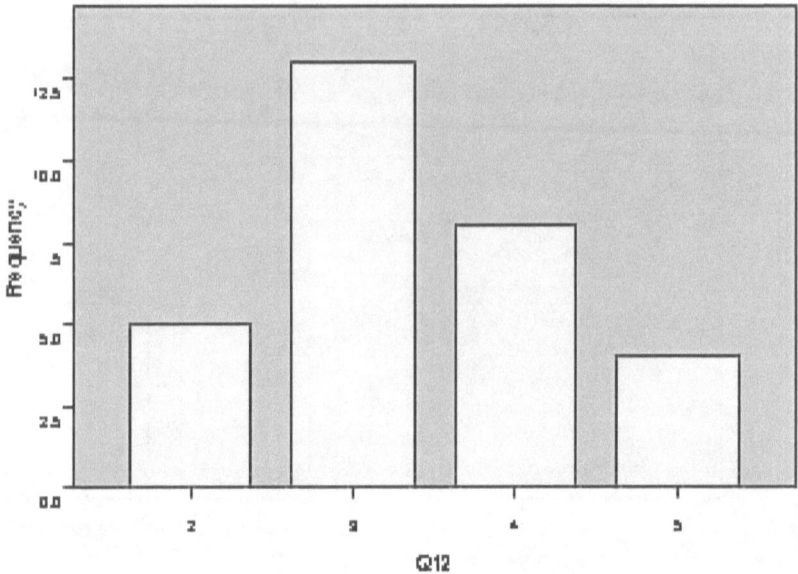

Figure 15. Question 12-Bar graph
2= Disagree to 5=Strongly Agree.

Bar graph – question 12 asked respondents whether or not *culture affects affordable housing.* Showed in bar graph, no respondents strongly disagreed, five respondents (16.7%) disagreed, 13 respondents (43.3%) were neutral, eight respondents (26.7%) agreed, and four respondents (13.3%) strongly agreed. Neutrality in the bar graph indicated that culture has no affects on affordable housing. Two experts disagreed and one expert was neutral when responding to survey question 12.

Survey question 13 asked respondents whether or not *electronic marketplaces affect affordable housing.* One respondent (3.3%) disagreed, 12 respondents (40%) were neutral, 14 respondents (46.7%) agreed, and three respondents (10%) strongly agreed. Question 13 had a mean of 3.63; a mode of 3, and a standard deviation of .72, indicating participants agreed that electronic marketplaces affect affordable housing (see Figure 16).

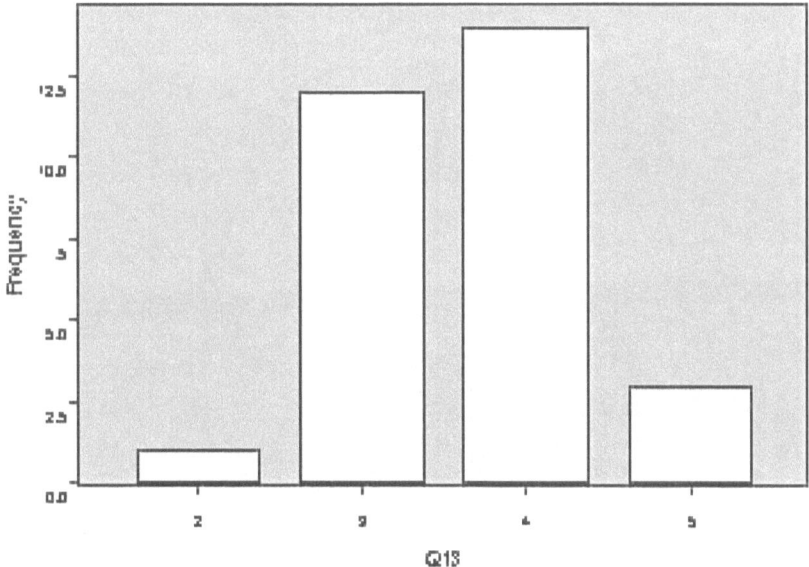

Figure 16. Question 13-Bar graph
2= Disagree to 5 = Strongly Agree.

Bar graph – question 13 asked respondents whether or not *electronic marketplaces affect affordable housing*. Indicated in the bar graph, one respondent (3.3%) disagreed, 12 respondents (40%) were neutral, 14 respondents (46.7%) agreed, and three respondents (10%) strongly agreed. Electronic marketplaces indicated in the bar graph have no strong affect on affordable housing. One expert disagreed, one expert was neutral, and one expert strongly agreed with survey question 13.

Survey question 14 asked respondents whether or not the *Nigerian governmental policies would lead to affordable housing.* Two respondents (6.7%) strongly disagreed, four respondents (13.3%) disagreed, 11 respondents (36.7%) were neutral, nine respondents (30%) agreed, and four respondents (13.3%) strongly agreed. Question 14 had a mean of 3.3, a mode of 3, and a standard deviation of 1.09, indicating a slight trend toward agreement on whether or not Nigerian governmental policies would lead to affordable housing (see Figure 17).

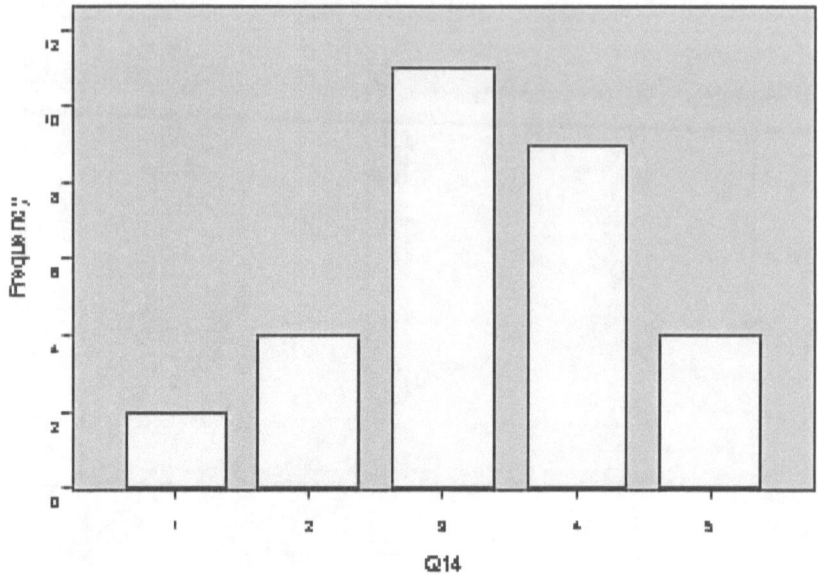

Figure 17. Question 14-Bar graph
1 = Strongly Disagree to 5 = Strongly Agree.

Bar graph – question 14 asked respondents whether or not the *Nigerian governmental policies would lead to affordable housing.* Explained in the bar graph, two respondents (6.7%) strongly disagreed, four respondents (13.3%) disagreed, 11 respondents (36.7%) were neutral, nine respondents (30%) agreed, and four respondents (13.3%) strongly agreed. Participants were neutral or agreed to the survey question as indicated in the bar graph. One expert strongly disagreed, one expert agreed, and one expert strongly agreed with survey question 14.

Survey question 15 asked respondents if *financial institution issuing low-interest loans affects affordable housing.* Three respondents (10%) strongly disagreed, four respondents (13.3%) disagreed, seven respondents (23.3%) were neutral, ten respondents (33.3%) agreed, and six respondents (20%) strongly agreed. Question 15 had a mean of 3.4, a mode of 4, and a standard deviation of 1.25, indicating a slight trend toward agreement that financial institutions issuing low-interest loans affects affordable housing (see Figure 18).

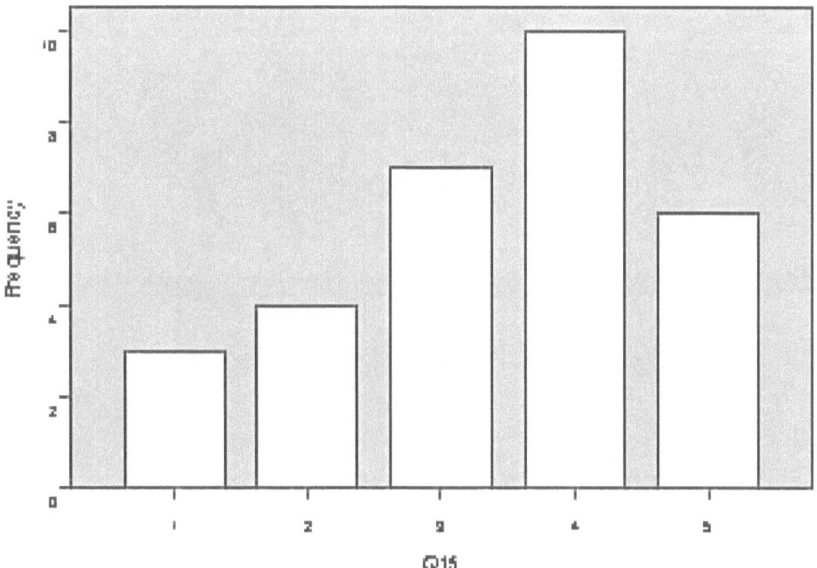

Figure 18. Question 15-Bar graph
1=Strongly Disagree to 5=Strongly Agree.

Bar graph – question 15 asked respondents if *financial institution issuing low-interest loans affects affordable housing.* Indicated in bar graph, three respondents (10%) strongly disagreed, four respondents (13.3%) disagreed, seven respondents (23.3%) were neutral, ten respondents (33.3%) agreed, and six respondents (20%) strongly agreed. Explained in the bar graph, participants generally agreed with the survey question that low-interest loan will affects affordable housing. Two experts agreed and one expert strongly agreed with survey question 15.

Survey question 16 asked respondents whether or not *you have had not too pleasant experience with affordable housing.* One respondent (3.3%) strongly disagreed, six respondents (20%) disagreed, 11 respondents (36.7%) were neutral, six respondents (20%) agreed, and six respondents (20%) strongly agreed. Question 16 had a mean of 3.33, a mode of 3, and a standard deviation of 1.24, indicating a slight trend toward agreement that participants have had a not too pleasant experience with affordable housing (see Figure 19).

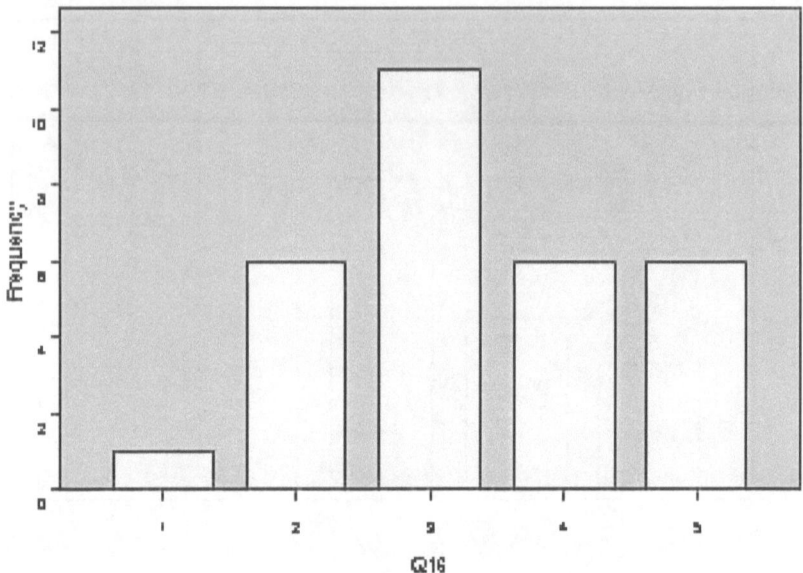

Figure 19. Question 16-Bar graph
1=Strongly Disagree to 5=Strongly Agree.

Bar graph – question 16 asked respondents whether or not *you have had not too pleasant experience with affordable housing.* Indicated in bar graph, one respondent (3.3%) strongly disagreed, six respondents (20%) disagreed, 11 respondents (36.7%) were neutral, six respondents (20%) agreed, and six respondents (20%) strongly agreed. Participants in the bar graph remained neutral or agreed with the survey question depending on perceived experience. Two experts were neutral and one expert agreed with question 16.

Survey question 17 asked respondents whether or not *Abuja city is not meant for the middle-income population.* No respondents strongly disagreed, one respondent (3.3%) disagreed, 17 respondents (56.7%) were neutral, eight respondents (26.7%) agreed, and four respondents (13.3%) strongly agreed. Question 17 had a mean of 3.5, a mode of 3, and a standard deviation of .78, indicating the majority was neutral, although 40% agreed or strongly agreed that Abuja city were not meant for the middle-income population (see Figure 20).

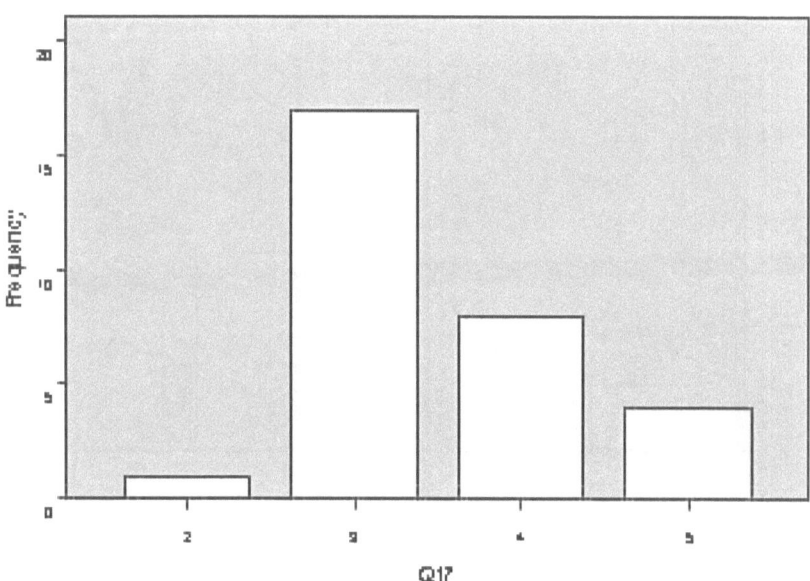

Figure 20. Question 17-Bar graph
2= Disagree to 5= Strongly Agree.

Bar graph –question 17 asked respondents whether or not *Abuja city was not meant for the middle-income population.* No respondents strongly disagreed, one respondent (3.3%) disagreed, 17 respondents (56.7%) were neutral, eight respondents (26.7%) agreed, and four respondents (13.3%) strongly agreed. Interpretation as showed in the bar graph depended on what middle-income population nebulously meant to the participants. Subsequently, participants remained neutral or tend to agree with the survey question. Two experts agreed and one expert strongly agreed with question 17.

Survey question 18 asked respondents if *expensive housing was available in Abuja.* Two respondents (6.7%) strongly disagreed, three respondents (10%) disagreed, 14 respondents (46.7%) were neutral, six respondents (20%) agreed, and five respondents (16.7%) strongly agreed. Question 18 had a mean of 3.3, a mode of 3, and a standard deviation of 1.09, indicating a slight trend toward agreement that expensive housing was available in Abuja (see Figure 21).

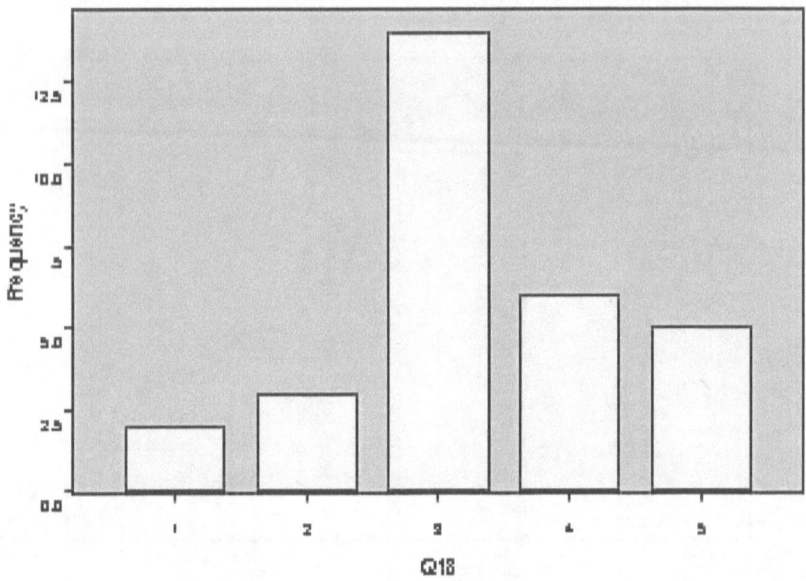

Figure 21. Question 18-Bar graph
1=Strongly Disagree to 5=Strongly Agree.

Bar graph – question 18 asked respondents if *expensive housing was available in Abuja*. Indicated in the bar graph, two respondents (6.7%) strongly disagreed, three respondents (10%) disagreed, 14 respondents (46.7%) were neutral, six respondents (20%) agreed, and five respondents (16.7%) strongly agreed. Explained in the bar graph participants were neutral, agreed or strongly agreeing with the survey question with few participants disagreeing. All three experts agreed with question 18.

Survey question 19 asked respondents if *you intend to live in the city*. One respondent (3.3%) strongly disagreed, four respondents (13.3%) disagreed, 12 respondents (40%) were neutral, eight respondents (26.7%) agreed, and five respondents (16.7%) strongly agreed. Question 19 had a mean of 3.4, a mode of 3, and a standard deviation of 1.09, indicating a slight trend toward agreement that participants intend to live in the city (see Figure 22).

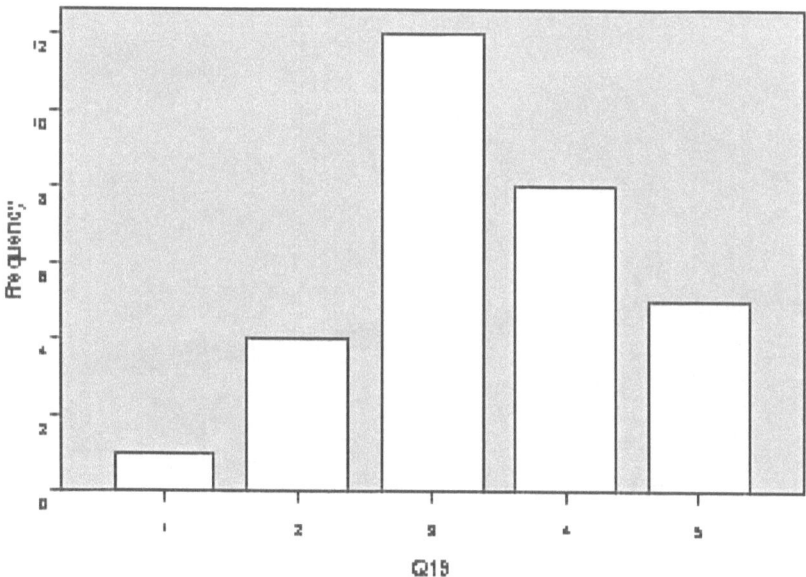

Figure 22. Question 19-Bar graph
1=Strongly Disagree to 5=Strongly Agree.

Bar graph – question 19 asked respondents if *you intend to live in the city.* Indicated in the bar that one respondent (3.3%) strongly disagreed, four respondents (13.3%) disagreed, 12 respondents (40%) were neutral, eight respondents (26.7%) agreed, and five respondents (16.7%) strongly agreed. Explained in the bar graph is that despite expensive housing in Abuja, participants remained neutral or showed willingness to live in the city. Two experts disagreed with question 19, and one expert was neutral.

Survey question 20 asked respondents if *information of affordable housing was centralized on a server.* Four respondents (13.3%) strongly disagreed, three respondents (10%) disagreed, eight respondents (26.7%) were neutral, 14 respondents (46.7%) agreed, and one respondent (3.3%) strongly agreed. Question 20 had a mean of 3.17, a mode of 4, and a standard deviation of 1.12, indicating a slight trend toward agreement that information of affordable housing was centralized on a server (see Figure 23).

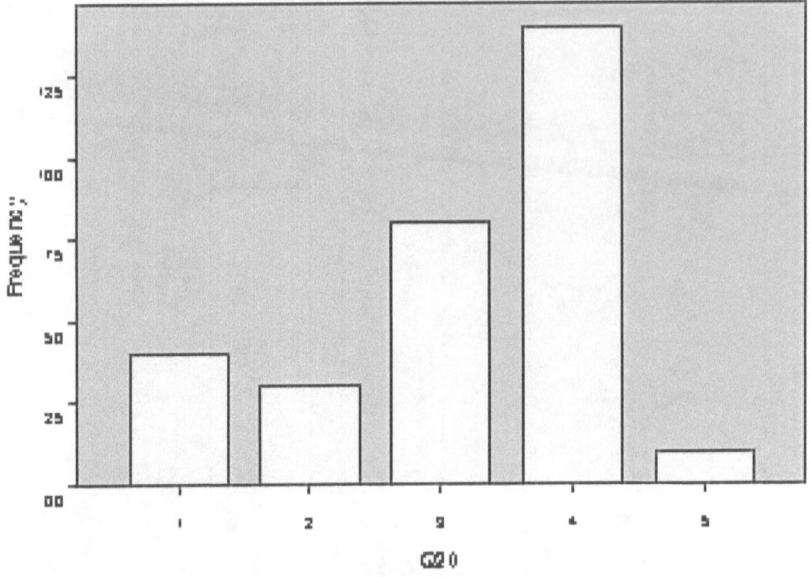

Figure 23. Question 20-Bar graph
1 = Strongly Disagree to 5 = Strongly Agree.

Bar graph – question 20 asked respondents if *information of affordable housing was centralized on a server.* Showed in the bar graph, four respondents (13.3%) strongly disagreed, three respondents (10%) disagreed, eight respondents (26.7%) were neutral, 14 respondents (46.7%) agreed, and one respondent (3.3%) strongly agreed. Participants in the bar graph remained neutral or agreed with the survey question. One expert strongly disagreed, one expert was neutral, and one expert agreed with question 20.

Survey question 21 asked respondents if *information on potential loan applications was available through Central Bank of Nigeria computer server.* Three respondents (10%) strongly disagreed, four respondents (13.3%) disagreed, ten respondents (33.3%) were neutral, ten respondents (33.3%) agreed, and three respondents (10%) strongly agreed. Question 21 had a mean of 3.2, a mode of 3, and a standard deviation of 1.13, indicating a slight trend toward agreement that information on potential loan applications was available through Central Bank of Nigeria computer server (see Figure 24).

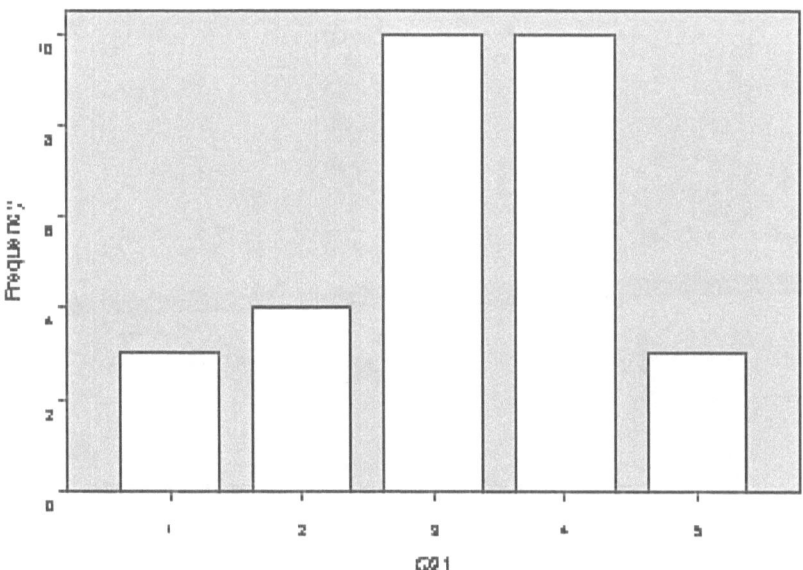

Figure 24. Question 21-Bar graph
1=Strongly Disagree to 5=Strongly Agree.
Bar graph – question 21 asked respondents if *information on potential loan applications was available through Central Bank of Nigeria computer server.* Explained in the bar graph, three respondents (10%) strongly disagreed, four respondents (13.3%) disagreed, ten respondents (33.3%) were neutral, ten respondents (33.3%) agreed, and three respondents (10%) strongly agreed. Explicated in the bar graph was neutrality and agreement amongst the participants to the survey question. One expert strongly disagreed and two experts strongly agreed with question 21.

Survey question 22 asked respondents whether or not *FCDA has a centralized server for houses that are affordable to the middle-income population.* Three respondents (10%) strongly disagreed, three respondents (10%) disagreed, nine respondents (30%) were neutral, 11 respondents (36.7%) agreed, and four respondents (13.3%) strongly agreed. Question 22 had a mean of 3.33, a mode of 4, and a standard deviation of 1.16, indicating a slight trend toward agreement that FCDA has a centralized server for houses that are affordable to the middle-income population (see Figure 25).

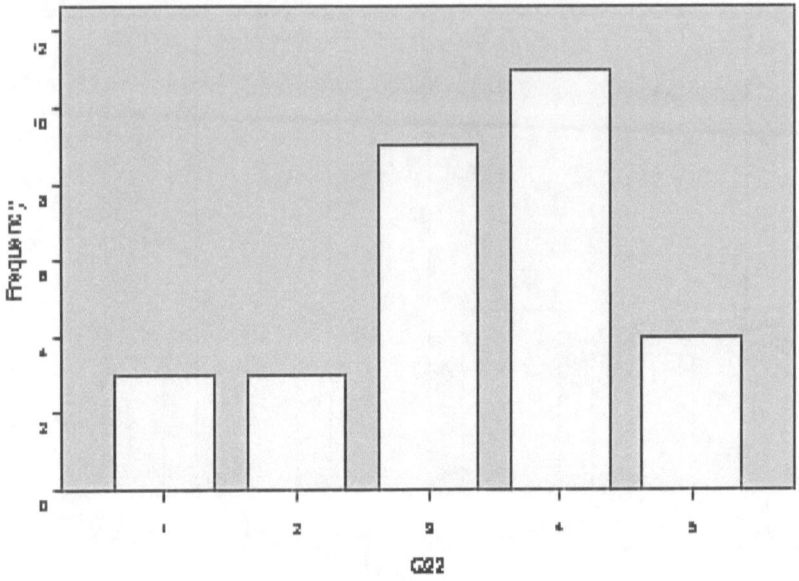

Figure 25. Question 22-Bar graph
1=Strongly Disagree to 5=Strongly Agree.

Bar graph – question 22 asked respondents whether or not *FCDA has a centralized server for houses that are affordable to the middle-income population.* Indicated in the bar graph, three respondents (10%) strongly disagreed, three respondents (10%) disagreed, nine respondents (30%) were neutral, 11 respondents (36.7%) agreed, and four respondents (13.3%) strongly agreed. Participants showed neutrality and agreement to the survey question as illuminated in the bar graph. Two experts were neutral and one expert strongly agreed with question 22.

Survey question 23 asked respondents if *banks store information on available housing in a centralized server.* One respondent (3.3%) strongly disagreed, eight respondents (26.7%) disagreed, ten respondents (33.3%) were neutral, four respondents (13.3%) agreed, and seven respondents (23.3%) strongly agreed. Question 23 had a mean of 3.27, a mode of 3, and a standard deviation of 1.20, indicating little agreement among participants whether or not banks store information on available housing in a centralized server (see Figure 26).

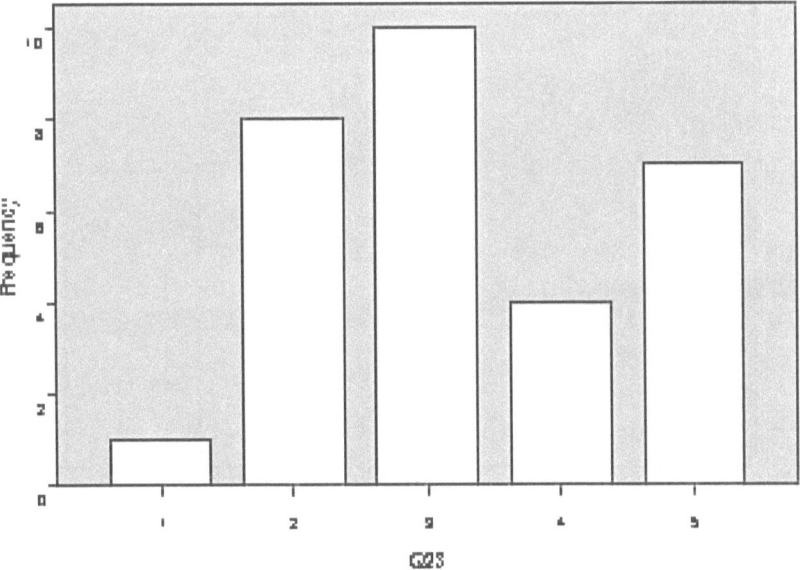

Figure 26. Question 23-Bar graph
1 = Strongly Disagree to 5 = Strongly Agree.

Bar graph – question 23 asked respondents if *banks store information on available housing in a centralized server.* Indicated in the bar graph, one respondent (3.3%) strongly disagreed, eight respondents (26.7%) disagreed, ten respondents (33.3%) were neutral, four respondents (13.3%) agreed. Participants explained various positions on the bar graph, from disagreement, neutral to agreeing with the survey question. All three experts disagreed with question 23.

Survey question 24 asked respondents if *the centralized server could be access by the private sector.* Two respondents (6.7%) strongly disagreed, two respondents (6.7%) disagreed, 12 respondents (40%) were neutral, eight respondents (26.7%) agreed, and six respondents (20%) strongly agreed. Question 24 had a mean of 3.47, a mode of 3, and a standard deviation of 1.11, indicating a slight trend toward agreement that the centralized server can be access by the private sector (see Figure 27).

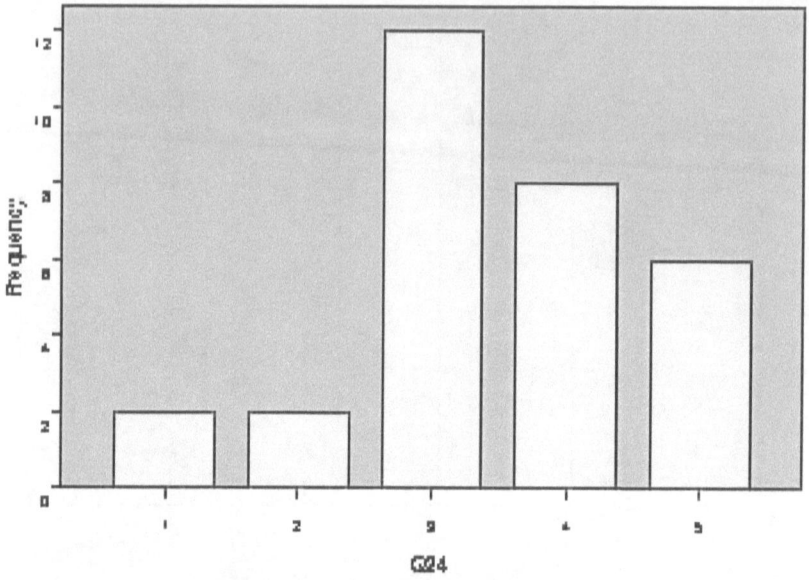

Figure 27. Question 24-Bar graph
1=Strongly Disagree to 5=Strongly Agree.

Bar graph – question 24 asked respondents if *the centralized server could be access by the private sector.* The bar graph indicated that two respondents (6.7%) strongly disagreed, 2 (6.7%) disagreed, 12 respondents (40%) were neutral, eight respondents (26.7%) agreed, and six respondents (20%) strongly agreed. Participants were neutral, agreed or strong agree with the survey question as explained in the bar graph. All three experts disagreed with question 24.

Survey question 25 asked respondents whether or not *there are no centralized servers.* Two (6.7%) strongly disagreed, five respondents (16.7%) disagreed, ten respondents (33.3%) were neutral, ten respondents (33.3%) agreed, and three respondents (10%) strongly agreed. Question 25 had a mean of 3.23, a mode of 3, and a standard deviation of 1.07, indicating a slight trend toward agreement of an existence of centralized servers (see Figure 28).

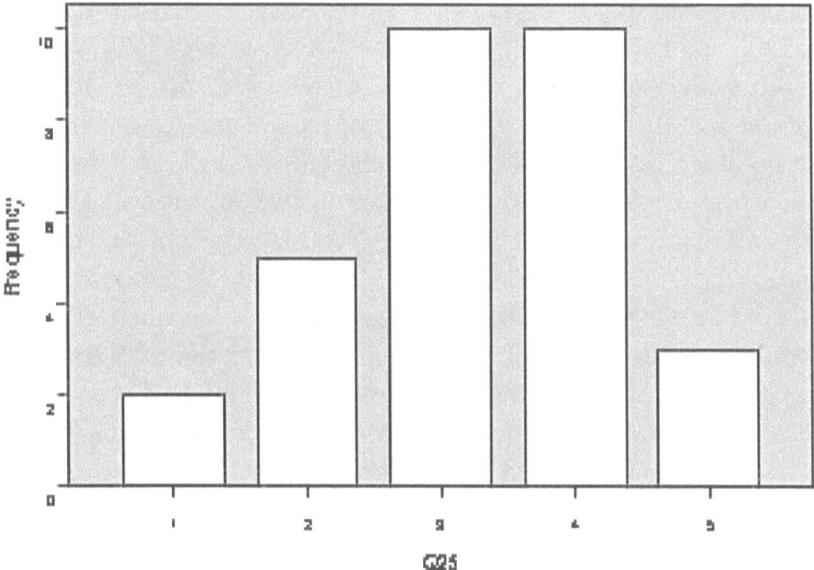

Figure 28. Question 25-Bar graph
1=Strongly Disagree to 5=Strongly Agree.

Bar graph – question 25 asked respondents whether or not *there are no centralized servers.* Indicated in the bar graph, two respondents (6.7%) strongly disagreed, five respondents (16.7%) disagreed, ten respondents (33.3%) were neutral, ten respondents (33.3%) agreed, and three respondents (10%) strongly agreed. Participants in the bar graph were neutral and agreeing to the survey question. One expert strongly disagreed and one expert disagreed with question 25.

SATURATION OF THE PHENOMENOLOGICAL STUDY

External validity for the study was limited because participant's responses might not reflect opinions from the entire middle-income population in Abuja (Neumann, 2003). Data might be misrepresented, misinterpreted, limited or misconstrued due to dearth of the sample population selected and methodology used. During official working hours, qualitative questionnaires were administered to participants. Some participants, in responding to the qualitative questions, omitted some questions for reasons beyond the scope of current study. Participants returned the questionnaires within one hour. When asked why the survey was not completed, participants responded that they only completed the sections of the survey that affected the middle-income population.

After the qualitative surveys were returned, all participants received and filled out the quantitative questionnaire. All quantitative questionnaires were completed and returned within four hours. The private sector participants said the quantitative survey was easier to fill out. Quantitative survey questionnaire analysis from participants supplemented and provided support for the qualitative responses.

In a phenomenological study, responses provided on questionnaires are subjective and based on the respondent's perspectives (Devers & Frankel, 2000). Quantitative survey questionnaire (see Appendix A) provided a process for sequential ordering and interpreting of the underlying themes. Experts in the field of real estate management, strategic policy planning, and finance were consulted to compare, collaborate, or refute information gathered from the respondents. Experts responded to the same quantitative questionnaire as the participants. Results from the experts primarily supported or rejected opinions and responses to questionnaires posed to the middle-income population respondents.

A phenomenological saturation of study was attained because responses gleaned from 30 participants became repetitive as guided by step two of the Moustakas (1994) modified van Kaam method of analysis. Step two specifics were "reduction and elimination of invariant constituents and repetitive responses" (p. 121). Due to the repetitiveness of similar key words and sentences in participant's responses, the need to further explore the phenomenon was terminated. Key words were coded into themes. Neumann (2003) noted that ten to 20 similar responses from participants could be used to establish a saturation point within a phenomenological qualitative study.

THEMES

Purpose of administering interview questions to participants was to discern the underlying themes or to find a thematic pattern within the phenomenon (Neumann, 2003; Simon, 2006). Quantitative findings were compared with that of qualitative in discerning the themes. Themes were discerned from participants' responses following the three core research interview questions.

Presentation of Results by Research Questions and Themes

The following three core research questions are investigated:

1. Based on your experiences, how does the lack of affordable housing affect the middle-income population in Abuja, Nigeria?

2. Based on your experiences, how does the Nigerian culture impact affordable housing and price of housing in Abuja?

3. Based on your experiences, how does technological information exchange within the stakeholders in Abuja result in availability of housing for the middle-income population?

RESEARCH QUESTION I

First research question was to purposefully determine how the lack of affordable housing affects the middle-income population in Abuja. The Central Bank of Nigeria (CBN) Employees, the Federal Capital Development (FCDA) employees, and the private sector employees responded to the question. Data collected were coded for privacy and confidentiality. A saturation point was obtained for validity because all participants responded similarly to both the qualitative question and quantitative survey. Theme that resonates from the respondents was *affordable housing.*

Theme 1: Lack of Affordable Housing

Affordable housing was a recurring theme from the participants. Participants stated that double digit interest rates and a low-income range contributed to the lack of affordable housing. Participant P5 (FCDA Engineer) explained," the income or salary for housing was not enough." Participant P2 (Builder) stated that "the middle-income earners are not welcome in Abuja due to the price attached to housing."

A lack of low interest loans impacts the middle-income population's standard of living. Loans are available to middle-income earners at double-digit figures. Participant F3 (FCDA Staff) supported the statement by stating that "financial institutions are doing nothing for the middle-income earners except for friends, and the interest rates on loans are high." A lack of lower interest rates on loans and the lack of a broader salary range are the sub-themes that affected affordable housing.

In qualitative questions 1, 4, and 6, affordable housing by the middle-income population was a recurring theme. In comparison, quantitative survey questions 1, 2, 3, 6, and 7 skewed towards agreeing or strongly agreeing with the participants. For example, Survey question one asked respondents if *affordable housing was core to a nation's development.* Nine respondents (30%) agreed with the statement and 21 (70%) strongly agreed with the statement. Question one had a mean of 4.7; a mode of 5, and a standard deviation of .46, indicating that the all the respondents agreed or strongly agreed that affordable housing was core to a nation's development. In comparison, the three experts all strongly agreed that affordable housing was core to a nation's development.

In the literature review, affordable housing for the middle-income population was core to a nation's development (Ibagere, 2002). According to Ibagere, housing for the middle-income population remained core to nation's infrastructure development. DeSoto (2000) noted that for any meaningful development to occur in developing nations housing schemes be inculcated into the infrastructure development.

Research Question 2

Second research question explored how the Nigerian culture impacts the price of housing in Abuja. Nigerian people, conjecturally, frowned upon institutional loans (Ayemi, 2001). FCDA staff member who participated and responded to survey question stated that people who obtained loans granted for personal residences might be financially insolvent. Based on participant's responses to this interview question, culture was a discerning theme.

Theme 2: The Nigerian Culture

According to Participant P5, within the 253 mixed ethnicities and languages, "culture has no impact on housing." General definition of culture within the context of study was subjectively divergent. Participants defined culture in Nigeria as both individualistic and collectivistic.

Results indicated that the Nigerian culture has no impact on the price of housing. Participants P7, P8, P9, F7, F8, F9, C7, C8, C9, and P5 all responded that the culture shaped how individuals interpret the difficulties associated with finding reasonable accommodations. Participant P2, a real estate developer for ten years, indicated, "culture has nothing to do one's ability to buy or lease reasonable accommodation in Abuja. That, finding reasonable accommodation should not be affront to the dignity of the middle-income population." According to C10, "seller prices or loans attached to houses available for lease or buy are subjective and has no cultural impact on the housing market." Participant P5 stated, "I feel the Nigerian culture has no bearing on one's ability to rent or buy a home. The most import thing was money. If I have the money, I can afford a nice house in Abuja."

In contrast to qualitative data, participants indicated that culture has no bearing on housing, survey question 12 asked respondents if *culture affects affordable housing.* Only five respondents (16.7%) disagreed, indicating that they did not believe culture affects affordable housing. Eight respondents (26.7%) agreed and four respondents (13.3%) strongly agreed. Quantitative data indicated participants were neutral or tended to agree that culture affects affordable housing. Two experts disagreed and one expert was neutral when responding to survey question 12.

Nigerian culture remained a divisive issue in the study because of the divergent ethnic groups (Appelbaum et al., 1998; Kanungo, 2001; Luthans, 2005; McNamara, 2001; Schein, 2004). According to Appelbaum et al., the internal and external factors emanating from the Nigerian culture could affect the lack of affordability of housing. For instance, Nigeria has over 350 languages and 250 ethnicities (Country Reports, Nigeria, 2004).

RESEARCH QUESTION 3

Third research question explored the affect of technological information exchange between stakeholders in Abuja. How information availability in FCDA or CBN centralized server on housing could enhance search of housing for the middle-income population was pertinent to this question. Participants referred to technological peripherals such as the internet, extranet, and intranet in their responses.

Theme 3: The internet, extranet, and intranet. Survey question ten asked respondents whether or not *the internet was important to affordable housing.* Six respondents (20%) strongly disagreed, six respondents (20%) disagreed, five respondents (16.7%) were neutral, four respondents

(13.3%) agreed, and nine respondents (30%) strongly agreed. There was little agreement on whether or not the internet was important to affordable housing.

Survey question 11 asked respondents if *communication was vital to affordable housing.* Participants tended to agree that communication was vital to affordable housing. Survey question 13 asked respondents whether or not *electronic marketplaces affect affordable housing.* Participants tended to agree that electronic marketplaces affect affordable housing. One expert disagreed, one expert was neutral, and one expert strongly agreed with survey question 13.

Individuals who were technologically literate responded to the research question on information technology. Participants P1, P2, P3, F1, F2, and F3 supported the idea that internet cafes or centers are available within reach of the middle-income population. The internet cafes are sparsely spread within the city. F2 (FCDA Staff) stated,

> "I think the internet will provide good information on housing but will not provide substantive information on affordability housing in Abuja. I do not think there is centralized information on housing (Participant F2)."

Participant P10 stated that it would be good to have all the information housing in a centralized server. A centralized server was not available yet in Abuja for the middle-income population to find available housing." The quantitative data did not indicate consensus on the existence of a centralized server. Survey question 20 asked respondents if *information of affordable housing was centralized on a server.* Question 20 had a mean of 3.17, a mode of 4, and a standard deviation of 1.12, indicating a slight trend toward agreement that information of affordable housing was centralized on a server. One expert strongly disagreed, one expert was neutral, and one expert agreed with question 20.

Survey question 21 asked respondents if *information on potential loan applications was available through Central Bank of Nigeria computer server.* There was a slight trend toward agreement that information on potential loan applications was available through Central Bank of Nigeria computer server. Survey question 22 asked respondents whether or not *FCDA has a centralized server for houses that are affordable to the middle-income population.* There was a slight trend toward agreement that FCDA has a centralized server for houses that are affordable to the middle-income population.

Survey question 23 asked respondents whether or not *banks store information on available housing in a centralized server.* Agreement among participants was not substantial as to whether or not banks store information on available housing in a centralized server. All three experts disagreed with question 23. Survey question 24 asked respondents if *centralized server could be access by the private sector.* A slight trend towards an agreement was that the centralized server could be access by the private sector. All three experts disagreed with question 24.

Survey question 25 asked respondents if *there are no centralized servers.* There was a slight trend toward agreement that there are no centralized servers. One expert strongly disagreed and one expert disagreed with question 25. Results indicate that overall, there was no consensus on the availability of technology, centralized servers, or electronic information available to make finding affordable housing

In the literature review, the fundamental tenet in communication was that the internet should replaced the traditional methods of gathering information, including locating the availability of housing and exchanging information on properties (Akpan, 2003; Mbeki, 1999; Norris, 2001; Phillips, 2002; Truong, 2004). Electronic marketplaces and the supply of electricity needed for housing transactions are sporadic (Adenikinju, 2003). Supply of electricity in Abuja that supports the communication systems was relevant to study.

Adenikinju (2003) reported that 20% to 30% of initial investments in the private sector were for procurement of materials to augment the supply of electricity. Fundamentally, a method for reporting the traditional housing inventory in an electronic marketplace was not available in Abuja. Electricity that supports the internet remained sporadic (Adenikinju, 2003). Another element that contributed to unavailability of an electronic marketplace was the lack of centralization of information on housing into a server in Abuja (Country Reports, Nigeria, 2004). Participant C1 (CBN employee) stated that "infrequent supply of electricity that supports the internet inhibits finding reasonable accommodation. Finding reasonable accommodation could take up to six months depending on the location or area of the city where homes are available."

Theme 4: Economic infrastructures

Supply of electricity in Abuja that supports communication infrastructures was infrequent. Communication linking stakeholders to affordable housing are constantly interrupted. Non-centralization of information on housing within FCDA or the CBN server inhibits finding availability housing. Within city, where information on housing are partially centralized into a particular server, the middle-income population have no access to the information due to infrequent supply of electricity (Adenikinju, 2003). Participants P8, P2, P10, F8, F9, F10, C8, C9, C10, and P9 stated that constant electricity supply would improve communication on housing availability due to the present internet and telecommunication infrastructures in the city. Individuals emphasized that a lack of proper infrastructure and information on availability of houses have led to dissemination of information through the traditional methods. Apparently, no specialized center or centralized computerized server that espoused information on housing data. According to P2 (Builder/Developer),

> "I do not see technology as being fully developed for housing transactions in Abuja. Electricity supply continuously interrupts communication. I believe it will be nice to have constant supply of electricity to support the internet usage."

Participant F2 (FCDA Staff) supported the use of internet. F2 stated that the "internet will provide good information on housing but will not provide substantive information on affordability housing in Abuja." The internet cafes or centers are available within reach of the middle-income population. Participants P8, P2, P10, F8, F9, F10, C8, C9, C10, and P9 concurred that the internet cafes, which are sparsely spread within the city, would help middle-income population locate available homes.

One of the themes discerned was the *lack of infrastructures* that supports and facilitates housing in qualitative survey question five. In comparison to the quantitative survey, question 11 asked respondents whether or not *communication was vital to affordable housing*. Respondents tend to agree or strongly agreed that communication was vital to affordable housing. Two experts strongly agreed, and one expert was neutral to the survey question.

For housing to be regarded as core to a nation's development, constant supply of electricity inculcated into the city infrastructure remained vital (Ibagere, 2002). Constant electricity would support centralization of information in an FCDA or the CBN server. The centralized server leads to the broker's model as stated in the literature review. In addition, the broker model create avenue for real estate brokers to place housing inventories in the electronic marketplaces for effective and efficient transactions (Afuah & Tucci, 2003; Gottschalk & Abrahamsen, 2002; Rappa, 2004).

SUMMARY

Data analysis from the qualitative questions (see Appendix B) revealed that housing is expensive and the middle-income earners are unable to afford reasonable accommodations. Data indicated that the culture of people in the city has no effects to whether or not middle-income populations are able to afford housing. Study indicated that the internet was available when searching for housing; the internet has no impact on affordability or availability of housing. Data suggested technology usage was not fully developed for housing transactions through the internet or other electronic marketplaces.

In the study, salary range of the middle-income population has a direct impact on affordability of the housing. For this study, stakeholders are profit driven; no embedded incentives for stakeholders to address housing needs for the middle-income earners. In addition, data conveyed that collaborative working synergies of the stakeholder would improve the lack of affordable housing for the middle-income earners. In compendium, the quantitative data and statistical analysis primarily supported and complemented findings from the qualitative questions

CONCLUSION

Chapter 4 analyzed the qualitative and quantitative data collected from those who responded to the questions. Deployed procedures used in collecting data and techniques used were stated. Collection processes and documentations of the results were aggregately reported in connection with the research questions. Chapter 4 started with administrating qualitative research questions, followed by the quantitative survey questionnaires to the participants. Chapter 4 also discussed and explained why housing shortage exists in Abuja.

Chapter 5 will provide the conclusions regarding the themes expressed across the data collected. Recommendations in respect to housing accommodation for the middle-income population would be offered. Chapter 5 will suggest areas that needed further study. How current study could impact other cities in the sub-Saharan African region will be explicated in Chapter 5.

CHAPTER 5:

CONCLUSIONS AND RECOMMENDATIONS

The purpose of this study was to explore the lack of affordable housing for the middle-income population in Abuja. A phenomenological qualitative study was explored through the "inductive experience" (Devers & Frankel, 2000, p. 2) of the middle-income population. For this study, part of the analytic process used the modified van Kaam methodology by Moustakas (1994). Chapter 5 presents an overview of the previous chapters and reiterates the purpose of the study, an overview of problem statement, responds to the problem, and significance of the study to leadership. Chapter 5 ends with areas for future studies, conclusion, and recommendations.

OVERVIEW OF CHAPTERS

Chapter 1 introduced and explained reasons for the study. The purpose of the phenomenological qualitative study was to understand how affordable housing affects the middle-income earners. Understanding the phenomenon under study required asking the core research questions:

1. Based on your experiences, does the lack of affordable housing affect the middle-income population in Abuja?

2. Based on your experiences, how does the Nigerian culture impact affordable housing and price of housing in Abuja?

3. Based on your experiences, how does technological information exchange between the stakeholders in Abuja result in availability of housing for the middle-income population?

To respond to the research questions, a qualitative methodology was appropriate for the study (Creswell, 2002; Neumann, 2003; Simon, 2006). A quantitative method used a Likert-type scale to support and complement qualitative responses from the inductive experiences of the respondents. One expert in real estate, financial and strategic planners agreed, disagreed, or remained neutral to responses from participants.

Literature reviewed in Chapter 2 discussed the Nigerian culture and values that influence the stakeholder's actions that in turn affect housing (Eccles & Wigfield, 2002; Kacena, 2002; Schein, 2004). Fisher and Urich's (1999) stakeholder theory explained the need for the Nigerian government, financial institutions, and private organizations to collaborate synergistically in the implementation of any social program. Literature reviewed included Smith's (1776/1976b) invisible hand theory, Maslow's (1943) self-actualization theory, and Herzberg's (1964) two-factor theory. Within Nigerian governmental policies, Ibagere (2002) offered insight into the failure of formal governmental housing decrees to establish affordable housing. Adenikinju (2003) noted that affordable housing remained a core infrastructure for the development of a nation.

Chapter 3 described the phenomenological methodology for the study. Instrument used for the study was a modified van Kaam method by Moustakas (1994). A qualitative phenomenological research design fulfills the research goals. Semi-structured interviews with three open-ended questions provided qualitative responses that explained the phenomenon. Similar questions that fall within the delimiters were equally administered to participants. A quantitative survey questionnaire provided demographic information and ranked opinions regarding the relevant variables in the topic of lack of affordable housing. .

In Chapter 4, the research questions guided the central themes of study. Qualitative responses from participants were supported by the quantitative statistical analysis from the survey questionnaires. Sample size consisted of 30 participants in Abuja, Nigeria. Three experts opinions in real estate, financial planning, and strategic planning were used to compare, collaborate or refute responses from participants.

Data was gathered in a centralized location in Abuja. Central Bank of Nigeria was the first location where data was collected, followed by Federal Capital Development Authority. Private sector employees participated in the study. Chapter 5 presents the significance of the study to leadership, area for future study, the conclusion and recommendations.

REVIEW OF THE PROBLEM STATEMENT

Affordable housing remained a problem to the middle-income population in Abuja, Nigeria, and a lack of affordable housing has contributed to a specific socioeconomic problem (Ayemi, 2001). Karley (2003) maintained that "higher interest rates attached to [the] loans," (p. 27) granted to middle-income earners through financial institutions have resulted in a housing shortage. Specifically related to the problem of the lack of affordable housing was the average income of Nigerians and the high interest rates applied to mortgages (Ayemi, 2001; Karley, 2003).

RESPONDS TO THE PROBLEM

Respondents explained why finding available housing to rent or buy in Abuja remained difficult. Participants' experiences in finding available housing are reflected in the responses. Moustakas (1994) explained that the experiences of the population under study might include subjective elements; internal validation became necessary through saturation of data. From the Central Bank of Nigeria, interviews and questionnaires were conducted, and respondents postulated that higher interest rate on loans affected the ability of the middle-income population to affordable housing. In the governmental agencies and private sector, employees who responded to the interview questions and rank the survey questionnaires proffered low-income was subjectively the reasons for the lack of affordable housing. Overall, housing was available for rent or buy, with the context of study, only the rich can afford decent houses in Abuja. Discussions of the research interview questions explained the thematic meanings within the phenomenon.

Themes from survey questions revealed that middle-income earners could not afford housing. A lack of information available on housing and the Nigerian culture does not impact the price of housing. Effective and efficient communication on affordable housing was a theme discerned from the study. Statistical analyses were used to support the themes of study. From the study, low wages affects the capacity of middle-income populations to lease or buy homes. Electricity supply and other economic characteristics or economic infrastructures that supported use of the internet and other electronic mediums of exchanges were sparsely available. The Nigerian government inability to provide inadequate infrastructures in Abuja to support the housing market cascades into having expensive houses that are beyond the reach of the middle-income populations. Consequently, the unaffordable housing significantly affects the standard of living of the middle-income populations.

SIGNIFICANCE OF STUDY TO LEADERSHIP

Significance of study was to inform Nigerian leaderships of the phenomenon of a lack of affordable housing (Bass, 1990; Wren, 1994). Study explained that housing for middle-income population was not affordable. In the literature review, there was a paradox of Nigeria being rich in oil, arable land, human capital, and still a poor nation (The World Bank Group, 2003). Essentially, Nigerian richness in oil wealth was only distributed to the very few. A lack of affordable housing was the first theme discerned from participants' responses. Housing should be affordable for the middle-income population if the wealth was properly distributed to the population. Three experts, one in real estate management, one in financial and one strategic planner agree, disagree, or remained neutral with the participants who responded to the survey questionnaire.

In the literature review, culture was defined as a set of assumptions, values, norms, and tangible signs or artifacts as well as the facilitation of people's intrinsic and extrinsic social behaviors, ethnicity, language, and subliminal coded messages within enterprises (Appelbaum, Shapiro, & Elbaz, 1998; Kanungo, 2001; Luthans, 2005; McNamara, 2001; Schein, 2004). The Nigerian culture was the second theme discerned from participants' responses. Participants' responses revealed that the Nigerian culture has no impact on affordable housing. Nigerian culture of transacting businesses in cash has no impact on affordable housing. For this study, suggestion to the Nigerian leadership would be to encourage financial institutions to create avenues for the middle-income population to have access to low-interest loans.

Availability of housing information imperatively impacted the middle-income population ability to rent. Third theme discerned from study was that the internet, extranet, and intranet should provide pertinent information on housing. One expert agreed and two experts strongly agreed with participants' responses that informative materials should be provided on available housing. Imperatively, the Nigerian banks should create a centralized server within the Central Bank of Nigeria (CBN) to verify credit, condition, capacity, collateral, and conditions for potential loan applicants (Karley, 2003). Significant literature materials regarding potential applicants' inability to access information loans from the financial institutions were discussed. Without applicants' information and housing information in a centralized server, information required for housing transactions will be impossible to attain. Paramount to the Nigerian leaderships is to significantly be aware of a CBN server linked to an existing Federal Capital Territory Authority (FCDA) server that would benefit the stakeholders. For any meaningful development to occur in Abuja, housing must be part of the infrastructure (Akinwale, 2004; Ibagere, 2002; World Bank Group, 2006). In the literature, housing development remained part of the overall infrastructure of a nation. A lack of proper telecommunication emanated from supply of electricity interruptions that supported the information system. Fourth theme discerned from participants' responses reflected the significance of infrastructure as it affected the middle-income population. For a nation to develop, proper infrastructure was pivotal.

Participant's responses to quantitative survey questions comparatively complemented the qualitative responses. As reflected in quantitative survey question regarding qualitative question five indicated that one respondent (3.3%) strongly disagreed, one respondent (3.3%) disagreed, eight respondents (26.7%) were neutral, 14 respondents (46.7%) agreed and six respondents (20%) strongly agreed. Question 11 had a mean of 3.77, a mode of 4, and a standard deviation of .94, indicated participants tended to agree that communication was vital to affordable housing.

All the respondents agreed or strongly agreed that affordable housing was core to a nation's development. In comparison, the three experts supported, remained neutral or refuted the notion that affordable housing was core to a nation's development. The Nigerian leadership awareness regarding the significance of infrastructure remained pivotal to complementing affordable housing for the middle-income population.

Externally, the International Monetary Fund, the World Bank Group, Habitat for Humanity, and the United Nations Educational, Scientific, and Cultural Organization (UNESCO) could benefit from the study and help raised awareness of the macroeconomic problems of housing in developing nations. For example, the World Bank Group could assist leaders of developing nations in reducing housing shortages by channeling economic aid through housing programs. Similarly, Habitat for Humanity could provide low-interest construction loans and build affordable homes for middle-income earners in developing nations (Habitat for Humanity, 2005). The International Monetary Fund could financially assist the stakeholders

AREA FOR FUTURE STUDY

Replication of study using sample frame from the Nigerian general population will be recommended. Current study could be used as an anchor for future research to understanding housing situations in other sub-Saharan African cities. The word [middle-income population] was nebulously defined because of the nuances or thresholds used to determine income and other incentives attached to the salary range of the middle-income population. Within developed and underdeveloped nations, middle income populations are present and thus open avenues for future research.

CONCLUSIONS

The study objectives explored the lack of affordable housing through perceptions of the middle-income populations. Responses and findings from the three interview questions, other interview questions, and quantitative survey questionnaires administered to the participants explained the themes within the phenomenon. Experts in real estate management, financial and strategic planners, agreed, disagreed, or remained neutral to participants' responses. Data collected were analyzed, interpreted and evaluated. For the Nigerian leadership, the data interpretations raised the awareness of the inability of middle-income populations to afford housing. To the middle-income earners, the interpretation of the data suggested that information on housing was sparsely available. A broader interpretation of the study means that housing accommodations are vital to the middle-income populations, and housing represents a nation's future core economic development and basic infrastructure.

RECOMMENDATIONS

Imperatively and most significantly, stakeholders working synergistically and collaboratively to reduce housing shortage is recommended. Stakeholders should have a linkage or connection through a centralized server. A telecommunication infrastructure that support CBN or FCDA centralized server will be a trajectory towards reducing housing problem. For example, a centralized server established in FTCA or the Central Bank of Nigeria linking housing profile and comparables with applicants' historical data are pivotal to addressing the phenomenon. With a centralized server as a conduit, employers could provide information on available housing that is subsidized to the middle-income employees. Governmental agencies in collaboration with the private sector could provide housing subsidies to supplement the middle-income population wages. Without proper infrastructure in developing nations to augment and enhance potential facilities to facilitate loans, no superior alchemy could be used as a conduit to provide loans to the middle-income earners. Hence, the provident recommendation is for governmental agencies to engage and form partnership with other stakeholders to provide loans to the middle-income earners.

Significantly, financial institutions should start granting low-interest construction or housing loans to the middle-income population in Abuja. Banks should form strategic partnerships with potential local lenders (Risby & Greco, 2003). Potential borrower's character test for a mortgage can easily be met through verifications. Local leaders can verify the five criteria's for granting loans, namely, credit, condition, collateral, capital, and capacity through a CBN centralized server. Loan grants to the middle-class population should be in collaboration with local, international, and global partners. For example, the International Monetary Fund, the World Bank Group, Habitat for Humanity, and the United Nations Educational, Scientific, and Cultural Organization (UNESCO) can collaboratively formed partnerships with the Nigerian local banks. Externally, the aforementioned partnership should be monitored. Loan grants monitoring requires honest, prudent, and transparent people to implement the program from proposal to fecundity. More importantly, collaborative and proliferated efforts of the stakeholders should be implemented. Transparency and accountability are pertinent ingredients to guiding the partnership collaborative efforts in enhancing housing for middle-income population.

Private sector that engages in the building of homes for the middle-income families should be restricted to agreeable profit margins. State governments should augment the disparity within the profit margins. With tax and other incentives embedded in the implementation of the housing program, the collaborative partners would be energized and be compelled to produce results. Results would lead to reduction in housing shortage and the creation of affordable housing for the middle-income population.

DEFINITION OF TERMS

This study explored the lack of affordable housing from the point of view of the middle-income population. Definitions of terms to clarify ambiguities resulting from potential misinterpretation of underlying meanings are discussed. Terms and phrases used in the study are defined as follows:

Affordable housing. Means the ability of the middle-income population to purchase a single-family residence (Akinwale, 2004).

Central Bank of Nigeria (CBN). The institution responsible for monetary and fiscal policies in Nigeria as well as policies affecting construction and mortgage loans granted, by other financial institutions (Aderibigbe, 2002).

Certificate of occupancy. A deed of trust on land that means the land is free from encumbrances (El Rufai, 2004).

Decrees. Decrees are enacted in Nigeria to facilitate and to help implement government programs. These decrees cut across bureaucratic processes in facilitating the actions of the government (Akinwale, 2004).

Electronic marketplaces. In electronic marketplaces, intermediaries are eliminated from transactions, and sellers and buyers exchange goods and services for a fee and payment (Nigerian National Information Technology Development Agency, 2002).

Federal Capital Development Authority (FCDA). The FCDA monitors housing units in Abuja (El Rufai, 2004).

Federal Housing Authority (FHA). The FHA is responsible for the construction of new houses in Abuja. The FHA grants loans up to 50% to homebuyers with interest rates ranging from 11% to 15%. The 50% deposit has to be in cash. The FHA in Abuja is responsible for the implementation and compliance of governmental housing policies in Abuja (Anugwom, 2001).

Financial institutions. The banks, mortgage companies, and other quasi-banks in Abuja that grant construction and mortgage loans to middle-income earners (Obadan, 2002).

Godfatherism. In Nigeria, lower-level employees often bypass immediate managers due to influence from a top executive. Employees' in similar situations received a higher position because of a relationship established with the top executive. Top executives mentoring lower-level employees are different (Brown, 2004).

Horizontal Integration: Means those financial institutions with similar interests, compositions and method of operations forming partnerships to granting loans to potential middle-income applicants.

Infrastructure. Electricity to support the internet, extranet, and intranet connectivity to independent server protocols (Adenikinju, 2003). The infrastructure also includes effective electronic communication among stakeholders, the supply of constant electricity, and enabling environments for the use of technology in Abuja.

Middle-income earners. Middle-income earners in Nigeria earn an average of $100 USD monthly although the amount can vary greatly and depends on whether or not the employer is a governmental agency, the private sector, or a financial institution. The $100 USD reflects cost and standard of living of the people in Abuja (*Country Reports, Nigeria,* 2004).

Middle-income population. Average income in Abuja depends on location, the nature of a job, and the agency or the employer; the average monthly middle income is estimated to be $100 USD (Ibagere, 2002; World Bank Group, 2006).

Ministry of Works and Housing Nigeria. The ministry responsible for construction of roads, governmental offices, and housing for government middle-income earners (Aderibigbe, 2002).

National Housing Policies (NHP). The organization responsible for the construction of housing units in Nigeria. Significance of the NHP was apparent during the creation of Abuja. NHP was created and promulgated through Decree Number 53 of 1989. The intention of the decree and the establishment of NHP were to formulate cohesive housing policies that would lead to housing accommodation for middle-income earners (Ibagere, 2002).

Naira. Nigerian official currency. The Nigerian currency exchange at 125 naira to one dollar (World Bank Group, 2006).

Private sector. Private enterprises or organizations located in Abuja that also conduct business globally (Ibagere, 2002).

Synergies. These are combined efforts of financial institutions, governmental agencies, and the private sector in reducing the housing shortage or creating affordable housing for the middle-income population in Abuja rather than one entity trying to solve the problem alone (Akinwale, 2004).

Vertical Integration: Refers to external financial institutions, agencies, foundations, and world organizations with similar interests in reducing housing shortages in alignment with local Nigerian institutions or governmental agencies to granting low interest loans to middle income populations.

Working synergies. According to Post, Preston, and Sachs (2002), working synergies of the stakeholders are timeliness of communication, honesty, completeness, empathy, and equity of treatment by the managerial leadership.

World Bank Group. The World Bank Group consists of 184 member countries of the International Bank for Reconstruction and Development and the International Development Association responsible for providing financial and technical assistance to developing countries. World Bank groups provide low-interest loans and grants to developing countries for housing and other infrastructure (World Bank Group, 2006).

REFERENCES

Adenikinju, A. F. (2003). Electricity Nigeria: Electricity failures manufacturing sector. *Energy Policy, 31*(14), 15-19.

Aderibigbe, J. O. (2002). The role of the financial sector in poverty reduction. *CBN Economic & Financial Review, 49*(4), 12-14. Retrieved December 2, 2005, from http://www.cenbank.org/documents/efr.asp

Afuah, A., & Tucci, L. (2003). *Internet business models and strategies.* New York: McGraw Hill.

Ahlawat, S. S., & Ahlawat, S. (2006, March). Competing in the global knowledge economy: Implications for business education. *Journal of American Academy of Business, 8*, 101-103.

Akinwale, J. A. (2004). *Accessing the national housing fund-loan scheme.* Retrieved December 20, 2004, from http://www.deltastate.gov.ng/accessing(nhf).htm

Akpan, P. I. (2003). *Toward a Nigerian information society: Information and communication technologies as tools for social economic development. A case study.* Unpublished master's thesis, University of Alberta, Alberta, Canada.

Al-Obaidan, A. M. (2002). Efficiency effect of privatization in the developing countries. *Applied Economics, 34*, 111–117.

Amit, R., & Zott, C. (2001). Value creation in E-business. *Strategic Management Journal, 23*, 493–520.

Andriof, J., Waddock, S., Husted, B., & Wells, R. B. (2002). *Unfolding stakeholder thinking: Theory, responsibility, and engagement.* Sheffield, UK: Greenleaf.

Annan, K. (2001, January). *Secretary-general calls on governments to do their part in bridging digital divide.* Retrieved December 21, 2004, from http://www.un.org /News/Press/docs/2001/sgsm7686.doc.htm

Anugwom, E. E. (2001). *Privatization of workers' provision: The national housing fund (NHF) scheme in Nigeria.* Tangier-Morocco: African Training and Research Center in Administration for Development.

Appelbaum, S., Shapiro, B., & Elbaz, D. (1998). The management of multicultural group conflict. *Team Performance Management, 5*(4), 1-18.

Ariba. (2000). *B2B-Marketplaces in the new economy* (Research report). Retrieved January 15, 2005, from http://www.ariba.com

Ayemi, M. A. O. (2001). *The empirical development of a disaggregated residential location model in Nigeria.* Ibadan, Nigeria: University of Ibadan.

Baron, D. P. (2003). *Business and its environment* (4th ed). Upper Saddle River, NJ: Pearson Prentice-Hall.

Barrera, A. (2001). Open markets and collective bargaining: mutual advantages in distress. *Labor Law Journal 52*, 41-43.

Bass, B. M. (1990). *Bass & Stogdill's handbook of leadership: Theory, research, and managerial applications* (3rd ed.). New York: Free Press.

Bayliss, K. (2002). Privatization and poverty: The distribution impact of utility privatization. *Annals of Public and Cooperative Economics, 73*, 603-625.

Beauchamp, T. L., & Bowie, N. (2004). *Ethical theory and business* (7th ed). Upper Saddle River, NJ: Pearson Prentice-Hall.

Becker, B. (2002, June). The alignment conference: A stakeholder's way to create a competitive advantage. *Creativity & Innovation Management, 11*, 115-121.

Bernstein, P. L. (1996). *The winds of the Greeks and role of the dice.* New York: Wiley.

Block, N., & Catfolis, T. (2001). B2B E-market places: How to succeed. *Business Strategy Review, 12*(3), 20-28.

Boswell, C., & Cannon, S. (2005). New horizons for collaborative partnerships. *Online Journal of Issues in Nursing, 10*, 75-80.

Bowditch, J. L., & Buono, F. (2001). *A primer on organizational behavior.* Hoboken, NJ: Wiley.

Broadbent, M., & Kitzis, S. E. (2004). *The new competencies in IT: Harvard business school working knowledge.* Retrieved December 28, 2004, from http://www. hbswk.hbs.edu

Brown, C. J. (2004). *Leadership in Nigeria: A case study of reality, challenge, and opportunity.* Doctoral dissertation, University of Phoenix.

Cascella, V. (2002). Effective strategic planning. *Quality Progress, 35*(11), 62-68.

Charmaz, K. (2006). *Constructing grounded theory: A practical guide through qualitative analysis.* Thousand Oaks, CA: Sage.

Charreaux, G., & Desbrieres, P. (2001). *Corporate governance: Stakeholder value vs. shareholder value.* Dijon, France: University of Bourgogne.

Chowdhury, S. (2002). *Organization 21C: Someday all organizations will lead this way.* Upper Saddle River, NJ: Prentice Hall.

Clinton, W. (2000, July 22). *From digital divide to digital opportunity: A global call to action.* Retrieved November 10, 2004, from http://www.clinton4.nara.gov

Cooper, D. R., & Schindler, P. S. (2003). *Business research methods* (8th ed.). New York: McGraw-Hill Higher Education.

Cortright, J. (2001). *New growth theory, technology and learning: A practitioner's guide.* Retrieved December 21, 2003, from http://www.wds.impresaconsulting.com

Country Reports, Nigeria. (2004, August). *The countries: Nigeria.* New York: The Economist Intelligence Unit.

Country Reports, Nigeria. (2006). *The countries: Nigeria.* New York: The Economist Intelligence Unit.

Creswell, J. W. (2002). *Educational research, planning, conducting, and evaluating quantitative and qualitative Research.* Upper Saddle River, NJ: Merrill Prentice Hall.

Dai, Q., & Kauffman, R. J. (2002). Business models for the internet-based B2B electronic markets. *International Journal of Electronic Commerce, 6*(4), 41-73.

Davila, A., Gupta, M., & Palmer, R. (2003). Moving procurement systems to the internet: adaptation and use of E-procurement technology models. *European Management Journal. 21,* 11-24.

Dearnley, J., & Feather, J. (2001). *The wired world: An introduction to the theory and practice of the information society.* London: Library Association.

DeSoto, H. (2000). *The mystery of capital: Why capitalism triumphs in the west and fails everywhere else.* New York: Basic Books.

Devers, K. L., & Frankel, R. M. (2000). Study design in qualitative research 2: Sampling and data collection strategies. *Education for Health, 13,* 262-263

Drucker, P. F. (1998). The next information revolution. *Forbes, 162*(4), 4-47.

Drucker, F., & Peters, T. (2002). Information technology. *Information Today, 19,* 1-3.

Duru, E. C. (1997). Internet connectivity in libraries and information centers. *Information Services & Use, 17,* 61-65.

Eccles, J. S., & Wigfield, A. (2002). Motivational beliefs, values, and goals. *Annual Reviews Psychology, 53,* 109-132.

Edna, U. M. (1997). The invisible hand and the cunning of reason. *Social Research, 58,* 429-454.

Ehikhamenor, F. A. (2003). *Information technology in Nigeria banks: The limits of expectation.* Ibadan, Nigeria: Africa Regional Center for Information Science, University of Ibadan.

Ekeogu, I. O. (2002). *A comparative study of the readiness of developing nations for the networked world: West Africa versus newly wired developing countries.* Unpublished dissertation, Capella University.

El Rufai, M. N. A. (2004, April 29). *National ministerial press briefing, the International Conference Centre Abuja.* Retrieved December 20, 2004, from http://www. nigeria.gov.ng

Elliott, J. E. (2000). Adam Smith's conceptualization of power, markets, and politics. *Review of Social Economy, 58,* 429-454.

Ferraro, G. P. (2002). *The cultural dimensions of international business.* Upper Saddle River, NJ: Prentice Hall.

Fisher, K. T., & Urich, P. B. (1999). Information dissemination and communication in stakeholders' participation: The Bohol-Cebu water supply project. *Asia Pacific ViewPoint, 40,* 251-269.

Franz, R. (2003). Herbert Simon: Artificial intelligence as a framework for understanding intuition. *Journal of Economic Psychology, 24,* 265-267.

Gadde, L. E., & Hakansson, H. (2001). *Supply of network.* New York: Wiley.

Gagnon, M. A., & Michael, J. H. (2003). Employee alignment at a wood manufacturer: An exploratory analysis using lean manufacturing. *Forest Products Journal, 53*(10), 24.

Garegnani, P. (1983). The classical theory of wages and the role of demand schedules in determination of relative prices. *American Economic Review, 73,* 309.

Gee, C., & Burke, M. E. (2001). Realizing potential: The new motivation game. *Management Decision, 39,* 131-136.

Gottschalk, P., & Abrahamsen, A. F. (2002). Plans to utilize electronic marketplaces: The case of B2B procurement markets in Norway. *Industrial Management & Data Systems, 30,* 325-331.

Groves, R. (2004). Challenges facing the provision of affordable housing in African cities. *Housing Finance International, 18*(4), 26-27.

Guillen, M. F., & Suarez, L. (2005). Explaining the global digital divide: Economic, political, and sociological drivers of cross national internet use. *Social Forces, 84,* 681-780.

Habitat for Humanity. (2005). *A brief introduction.* Retrieved November 28, 2005, from http://www.habitat.org

Hair, J., & Bush, R. (2003). *Marketing research: Within a changing information environment.* Boston: McGraw Hill.

Hanley, S. J., & Abell, S. C. (2002). Maslow and relatedness: Creating an interpersonal model of self-actualization. *Journal of Humanistic Psychology, 42,* 37-57.

Herzberg, F. (1964). The motivation-hygiene concept and problems of manpower. *Personnel Administrator, 27,* 3-7.

Hollenbeck, J. R. (2000). A structural approach to external and internal person team fit. *Applied Psychology, 49*(3), 9-14.

Huang, G. L., Chang, H. C., & Yu, C. H. (2006). A comprehensive study on information asymmetry phenomenon of agency relationship in the banking industry. *Journal of American Academy of Business, 8*(2), 91-97.

Ibagere, O. P. (2002). *The dividend of democracy - How far with housing for all.* Presented at the Delta State Government Seminar at Asaba on the National Housing Fund, Asaba, Nigeria. Retrieved December 28, 2004, from http://www. deltstate.gov.ng

Ikejiofor, U. (1998). Access to land, development control and low-income housing in Abuja, Nigeria: Policy, politics and bureaucracy. *Planning and Practice & Research, 13*, 299-309.

Jones, G. R. (2003). *Organization theory, design, and change: Text and cases* (4th ed.). Upper Saddle River, NJ: Prentice-Hall.

Jonker, J., & Foster, D. (2002). Stakeholder excellence? Framing the evolution and complexity of a stakeholder perspective of the firm. *Corporate Social Responsibility and Environmental Management, 9*, 187-195. Retrieved December 25, 2005, from http://www. apollolibrary.com/Library/ERR/errReadings1.aspx

Kacena, J. F. (2002). New leadership directions. *Journal of Business Strategy, 23*, 21-23.

Kagitcibasi, C. (2001). *Individualism and collectivism: International differences in work related values.* Beverly Hills, CA: Sage.

Kanungo, R. N. (2001, December). *Ethical values of transactional and transformational leaders.* Canada: Administrative Sciences Association of Canada.

Karley, K. N. (2003) Challenges in mortgage lending for the under served in South Africa. *Housing Finance International, 18*, 27-29.

Kenny, C. (2002). *Information and communication technologies for direct poverty alleviation: Cost and benefits.* Malden, MA: Blackwell.

Khalil, T. M., & Hazem, A. (2005). Management of technology and responsive polices in a new economy. *International Journal of Technology 32*, 88-111.

Klein, S. (2003). The natural roots of capitalism and its virtues and values. *Journal of Business Ethics, 45*(4), 1-3.E10.

Kubasek, N. K., Brennan, B. A., & Browne, M. N. (2003). *The legal environment of business: A critical thinking approach* (3rd ed.). Upper Saddle River, NJ: Prentice Hall.

Lafferty, B. A., Goldsmith, B. A., & Newell, R. E. (2002). The dual credibility model: The influence of corporate and endorser credibility on attitudes and purchase intentions. *Journal of Marketing and Theory, 10*(3), 1-5.

Le, T. T. (2002). Pathways to leadership for business-to-business electronic marketplaces. *Electronic Markets, 12*(2), 12-120.

Lipis, L. J., Villars, R., Byron, D., & Turner, V. (2000). *Putting market into place: An e-marketplace. Definition and forecast* (IDC Research Report). Retrieved January 14, 2005, from http://www.idc.com

Luthans, F. (2005). *Organizational behavior* (10th ed.). New York: Irwin McGraw-Hill.

Malone, T. W., Yates, J., & Benjamin, R. I. (1989). The logic of electronic markets. *Harvard Business Review, 06/07,* 166-172.

Mangelsdorff, A. D. (2001). *Organizational behavior and theory.* Retrieved March 18, 2004, from http://www.txdirect.net/users/dmangels/orgbeh.htm

Maslow, A. H. (1943). A theory of human motivation. *Psychological Review, 50,* 370-396.

Matteson, T. M., & Ivanevich, J. M. (1999). *Management and organizational behavior classics* (7th ed.). New York: Irwin McGraw-Hill.

Mbeki, T. M. (1999, November 9). *The global information infrastructure: What is at stake for the developing world?* Retrieved December 21, 2003, from http://www.infodev.org

McNamara, C. (2001). *What is culture?* Retrieved February 2, 2005, from http://www.mapnp.org/library/org_thry/culture/culture.htm

Mintzberg, H., Lampel, J., Quinn, J. B., & Quinn, G. S. (2003). *The strategy process: Concepts, contexts, cases* (4th ed.). Upper Saddle River, NJ: Prentice Hall.

Moldoveanu, M., & Martin, R. (2001). *Agency theory and the design of efficient governance mechanisms.* Retrieved September 10, 2005, from http://www. rotman.utoronto.ca/rogermartin/Agencytheory.pdf

Moore, L. (2002). Online sales rise, but many buyers wary. *Customer Relationship Management Research Report,* 4–23. Retrieved December 21, 2003, from http://www.crmdaily.com

Moustakas, C. (1994). *Phenomenological research methods.* Thousand Oaks, CA: Sage.

Neumann, W. L. (2003). *Social research method: Qualitative and quantitative approaches* (4th ed.). Boston: Pearson Education.

Newan, I., Ridenour, C. S., Newman, C., & DeMarco, G. M. (2003). A typology of research purposes and its relationship to mixed methods. In A. Tashakkori & C. Teddie (Eds.), *Handbook of mixed methods in social & behavioral research* (pp. 167-188). Thousand Oaks, CA. Sage.

Newstrom, W. J., & Davis, K. (2002). *Organizational behavior: Human behavior at work.* New York: Irwin McGraw-Hill.

Nigeria Central Bank. (2005, June). *Annual report and statement of accounts.* Retrieved October 22, 2005, from http://www.cenbank.org

Nigerian National Information Technology Development Agency. (2002, January). *UNESCO: ICT-Cutting Theme* (Policy paper). Abuja, Nigeria: Author. Retrieved December 20, 2004, from http://www.portal.unesco.org/en/ev

Norris, P. (2001). *Digital divide: Civic engagement, information poverty, and the internet worldwide.* Cambridge, UK: Cambridge University Press.

Nutt, P. C. (2004). Expanding the search for alternatives during strategic decision-making. *Academy of Management Executive, 18*(4), 13-28.

Obadan, M. I. (2002). Poverty reduction in Nigeria: The way forward. *CBN Economic and Financial Review, 39*(4), 1-3. Retrieved December 2, 2005, from http://www. cenbank.org/documents/efr.asp

Ojide, D. C. (2003). *The factors that determine direct investment in Nigeria* [Dissertation abstract]. Sarasota, FL: University of Sarasota.

Osili, U. O. (2004). *Migrants housing investment: Theory and evidence from Nigeria.* Unpublished dissertation, University of Chicago.

Page, T. L. (2004). *A phenomenological study of female executives in information technology in the Washington, D.C.* Unpublished dissertation, University of Phoenix.

Payne, A., Christopher, M., Clark, M., & Peck, H. (2000). *Relationship marketing for competitive advantage: Wining and keeping customers.* Boston: Butterworth-Heinemann.

Peter, J. P., & Donnelly, J. H. (2003). *A preface to marketing management* (9th ed.). New York: Irwin McGraw-Hill.

Phillips, T. (2002). *Bulletin* interview: Larry Ellison. *Computer Bulletin, 07*(44), 4-6.

Pindyck, R., & Rubinfeld, D. (1989). *Microeconomics.* New York: Macmillan.

Porter, M. (1990). *The competitive advantage of nations.* New York: Free Press.

Post, J. E., Preston, L. E., & Sachs, S. (2002). Managing the extended enterprise: The new stakeholder view. *California Management Review, 45,* 6-28.

Rappa, M. (2004). Business models on the Web. *Managing the digital enterprise.* Retrieved January 28, 2004, from http:// digitalenterprise.org/models/models.html

Ricardo, D. (1961). *The works and correspondence of David Richardo.* Cambridge, UK: Cambridge University Press.

Salkind, N. J. (2003). *Exploring research* (5th ed.). Upper Saddle River, NJ: Prentice Hall.

Schein, E. (2004). *Organizational culture and leadership* (3rd ed.). San Francisco: Jossey-Bass.

Schermerhorn, J. R., Hunt, J. G., & Osbuorn, R. N. (2003). *Core concepts of organizational behavior.* Hoboken, NJ: Wiley.

Scott, R. W. (2003). *Organizations: Rational, natural, and open systems.* Upper Saddle River, NJ: Prentice Hall.

Simon, M. K. (2006). *Dissertation and scholarly research: A practical guide to start and complete your dissertation, thesis, or formal research project.* Dubuque, IA: Kendall/Hunt.

Smith, A. (1976a). *An inquiry into the nature and causes of the Wealth of Nations.* Chicago: University of Chicago Press. (Original work published 1776).

Smith, A. (1976b). *The wealth of nations.* Oxford: Clarendon Press. (Original work published 1776).

Strange, J. (2005). The dark side of organizational behavior. *Personnel Psychology, 58,* 531-532.

Strong, K. C., Ringer, R. C., & Taylor, S. A. (2001). THE* rules of stakeholder satisfaction (*Timeliness, honesty, empathy). *Journal of Business Ethics, 32*(3), 219-221.

Sumerlin, J. R. (1997). Self-actualization and hope. *Journal of Social Behavior & Personality, 12*(4), 1-10.

Taylor, R. W. (2000). *Urban development policies in Nigeria: Planning, housing, and land policy.* Upper Montclair, NJ: Montclair State University Center for Economic Research on Africa.

Tortola, J. O. (2001). It's the people, stupid. *Supermarket Business, 56*(2), 82-84.

Trigg, B. A. (2004). Deriving the Engel curve: Pierre Bourdieu and the social critique of Maslow's hierarchy of needs. *Review of Social Economy, 62*(3), 1-6.

Truong, D. (2004). *A study of business-to-business electronic marketing usage from the buyer perspective.* Unpublished dissertation, University of Toledo.

Turban, E., Lee, J., King, D., & Chung, M. (2000). *Electronic commerce: A management perspective.* Upper Saddle River, NJ: Prentice Hall.

Turner, S. (2002). *Organizational change.* Retrieved September 17, 2005, from http://faculty.fuqua.duke.edu/~willm/Classes/PhD/PhD_W02/Class02/Lit_Turner.doc

White, C. T. (2005). *Nigeria: Our world.* Retrieved October 22, 2005, *3,*2-4.

Wolverton, M. L. (2003). The mystery of capital: Why capitalism triumphs in the west and fails everywhere else. *Appraisal Journal, 71,* 272-274.

World Bank Group. (2000). *Nigeria financial sector review.* Washington, DC: World Bank Group, Economic Management and Social Policy Department, Financial Sector Unit.

World Bank Group. (2003). *International Bank for Reconstruction and Development (IBRD) member.* Retrieved December 22, 2005, from http://web.wordlbank.org

World Bank Group. (2006). *International Bank for Reconstruction and Development (IBRD) member.* Retrieved May 12, 2006, http://web.worldbank.org/wbsite/external/countries /africaext/ nigeriaextn/0,,menuPK:368906~pagePK: 141132~piPK:141107~t heSitePK:368896,00.html

Wren, D. A. (1994). *The evolution of management thought.* New York: Wiley.

APPENDIX A:

QUESTIONNAIRE

A Survey of Housing in Abuja

You are invited to participate in this survey because you are an employee of a financial institution, governmental agency, or a private enterprise. As a middle-income earner, your experience on how affordable housing affects you is solicited. Your information will be kept confidential. The information on names, other confidential matters will not be reveal to anyone without your express permission.

Name_____   Date_____

Gender: Female   Male   Age

Telephone No.   Email

Address

Employer: Financial institution   Governmental Agency

Private

Please check the box that may reflects your monthly salary range

1)   (N10, 000-N50, 000) 2)   (N50, 000-N75, 000)

3)   (N75, 000-N125, 000) 4)   (N125, 000 and above).

In the questions below: 1) means strongly disagree, 2) disagree, 3)

Neutral, Disagree, 4) Agree, 5) Strongly Agree.

	Strongly Disagree	Disagree	Neutral	Agree	Strongly Agree
1. Affordable housing is core to a nation's development	1	2	3	4	5
2. Affordable housing to middle-income population is part of a nation's infrastructure	1	2	3	4	5
3. Affordable housing does not affect me	1	2	3	4	5
4. Housing is subsidized through my employer	1	2	3	4	5
5. There are no middle-income earners in Abuja	1	2	3	4	5
6. Only the rich can afford housing	1	2	3	4	5

	Strongly Disagree	Disagree	Neutral	Agree	Strongly Agree
7. Without low-interest loans, there will be no affordable housing.	1	2	3	4	5
8. There is a housing shortage.	1	2	3	4	5
9. Housing accommodation are available.	1	2	3	4	5
10. The internet is important to affordable housing.	1	2	3	4	5
11. Communication is vital to affordable housing.	1	2	3	4	5
12. Culture affects affordable housing.	1	2	3	4	5
13. Electronic marketplaces affect affordable housing.	1	2	3	4	5
14. Nigerian governmental policies will lead to affordable housing.	1	2	3	4	5

15. Financial institution issuing low-interest loans affects affordable housing.	1	2	3	4	5
16. You have had not too pleasant experience with affordable housing	1	2	3	4	5
17. Abuja city is not meant for the middle-income population.	1	2	3	4	5
18. Expensive housing is available in Abuja.	1	2	3	4	5
19. Do you intend to live in the city?	1	2	3	4	5
20. Information of affordable housing is centralized in a server.	1	2	3	4	5
21. Information on potential loan applicants is available through Central Bank of Nigeria computer server.	1	2	3	4	5

	Strongly Disagree	Disagree	Unsure	Agree	Strongly Agree
FCDA has a centralized server for houses that are affordable to the middle-income population	1	2	3	4	5
Banks store information on available housing in a centralized server.	1	2	3	4	5
The centralized server can be access by private sector	1	2	3	4	5
There are no centralized servers	1	2	3	4	5

APPENDIX B:

QUALITATIVE INTERVIEW QUESTIONS

PLEASE ANSWER THE QUESTIONS BELOW:

1. Based on your experiences, how does the lack of affordable housing affect the middle-income population in Abuja, Nigeria?

2. Based on your experiences, how does the Nigerian culture impact affordable housing and price of housing in Abuja?

3. Based on your experiences, how does technological information exchange between the stakeholders in Abuja result in availability of housing for the middle-income population?

OTHER INTERVIEW QUESTIONS:

4. How do you feel about housing availability and affordability for the middle-income population?

5. How do describe financial institutions capacity to establish low-interest construction and mortgage loans to middle-income earners in Abuja?

6. How would you describe the private sector relative to affordable housing to employed middle-income earners?

7. How does communication in your organization improve housing availability or affordability for the middle-income population?

8. How will an electronic marketplace provide information on housing to the middle-income population?

9. How would you describe the effect of culture on governmental housing policies?

10. How would you describe culture with respect to housing within the private sector?

11. How do you describe partnerships and stakeholders in the housing market?

12. What is your experience with housing accommodation in Abuja?

APPENDIX C:
INFORMED CONSENT FORM
Consent to Act as a participant form

Participant,

I, _____ , will volunteer for this qualitative phenomenological study. I understand that participation is strictly my decision. I also understand that:

1. I may refuse to participate and/or withdraw at any time.

2. Research records and list of interviewees will be confidential.

3. Personal anonymity will be guaranteed.

4. Results of the general research data may be used for presentation and publications.

5. As the data is presented, I can choose to be identified as the source of that information for group discussion purposes.

6. _____ (researcher) has explained the study to me and answered my questions. If I have other questions or research related issues, I can be reached through/at _____.

There are no other agreements, written or verbal, related to the study beyond that expressed in the consent and confidentiality form.

By signing the form I acknowledge that I understand the nature of the study, the potential risks to me as a participant, and the means by which my identity will be kept confidential. My signature on the form also indicates that I am 18 years old or older and that I give my permission to voluntarily serve as a participant in the study described.

The participant shall return an executed form through email jparadigm @ aol.com or mail back the completed form in the enclosed self-addressed stamped envelope. The executed permission must be received prior to any interviews with the participant.

Signature of interviewee _____ Date_____

Signature of the researcher_____ Date_____

APPENDIX D:

LETTER OF INTRODUCTION

Dear Amina Salihu,

I am a student at the University of Phoenix working on a Doctor in Business Administration. I am conducting a research study entitled (Economic Characteristics Affecting Affordability and Shortages of Housing in Abuja, Nigeria). The purpose of the research study is to collect primary and secondary information that reflects situation of a housing shortage and a lack of affordable housing for the middle-income earners in Abuja. Alternatively, researcher will uncover that shortages housing do not exist in Abuja. Further, data analyses will unprejudiced-housing information in Abuja.

Nature of study is to gather primary and secondary data to elucidate why the stakeholders' integration of information into a centralized location is a risk reduction mechanism to middle-income population in Abuja. With integration of technological information in conjunction with stakeholder's functions, availability, affordability, or shortage of homes could easily be accessible by middle-income population in Abuja.

Your participation will involve answering ten potential structured interviews in Abuja. Researcher will carry out interviews to ascertain what role culture, values, and income play in creating a housing shortage in Abuja. Alternatively, the interviews may lead to the null hypothesis, thus showing that culture or ethnicity plays no crucial roles in creating a housing shortage in Abuja. Your participation in this study is voluntary. If you choose not to participate or to withdraw from the study at any time, you can do so without penalty or loss of benefit to yourself. The results of the research study may be published but your name will not be used and your results will be maintained in confidence.

In this research, there are no foreseeable risks to you.

Although there may be no direct benefit to you, the possible benefit of your participation is that at the conclusion of gathering primary and secondary data, information will be analyzed, synthesized, amalgamated, and triangulated by distilling factors that could be used to reduce the housing shortage in Abuja.

If you have any questions concerning the research study, please call me at 714-528-1063 or 011-234-9-5200768

An anonymous completed questionnaire will be considered as part of the subject's consent to participate and will be published.

Sincerely,

Joseph Aluya

Dear Sir,

I am a student at the University of Phoenix working on a Doctor in Business Administration. I am conducting a research study entitled (Economic Characteristics Affecting Affordability and

Shortages of Housing in Abuja, Nigeria). The purpose of the research study is to collect primary and secondary information that reflects situation of a housing shortage and a lack of affordable housing for the middle-income earners in Abuja. Researcher intends to uncover how governmental policies', financial institutions', and the private organizational sectors' functions are leading to a lack of affordable housing or a shortage of housing in Abuja will be focus of study. The operational term with Central Bank will be elevation of poverty through mitigating financial institution's risks in mortgage loans to middle-income earners.

Nature of study is to gather primary and secondary data to elucidate why the stakeholders' integration of information into a centralized location is a risk reduction mechanism to middle-income population in Abuja. With integration of technological information in conjunction with stakeholder's functions, availability, affordability, or shortage of homes could easily be accessible by middle-income population in Abuja.

Your participation will involve answering ten potential structured interviews in Abuja. Researcher will carry out interviews to ascertain what role culture, values, and income play in creating a housing shortage in Abuja. Alternatively, the interviews may lead to the null hypothesis, thus showing that culture or ethnicity plays no crucial roles in creating a housing shortage in Abuja. Your participation in this study is voluntary. If you choose not to participate or to withdraw from the study at any time, you can do so without penalty or loss of benefit to yourself. The results of the research study may be published but your name will not be used and your results will be maintained in confidence.

In this research, there are no foreseeable risks to you.

Although there may be no direct benefit to you, the possible benefit of your participation is that at the conclusion of gathering primary and secondary data, information will be analyzed, synthesized, amalgamated, and triangulated by distilling factors that could be used to reduce the housing shortage in Abuja.

If you have any questions concerning the research study, please call me at 714-528-1063 or 011-234-9-5200768

An anonymous completed questionnaire will be considered as part of the subject's consent to participate and will be published.

Sincerely,

Joseph Aluya

www.ingramcontent.com/pod-product-compliance
Lightning Source LLC
Chambersburg PA
CBHW061257280526
45784CB00002B/796